Serpents of Circe

Also in this series:

The New Aradia:
A Witch's Handbook to Magical Resistance
(Revelore Press, 2018)

The Gorgon's Guide
to Magical Resistance
(Revelore Press, 2022)

Serpents of Circe
A Manual to Magical Resilience

Edited by
Laura Tempest Zakroff
& Ron Padrón

Revelore Press
Olympia, WA
2024

Serpents of Circe: A Manual to Magical Resilience

© REVELORE PRESS 2024.
All contributors retain copyright to their individual works.

All rights reserved. No part of this publication may be reproduced or utilized in any form or by any means, electronic or mechanical, including photocopying, recording, or by any information storage and retrieval system, without permission in writing from the Publishers.

The authors and publisher assume no responsibility for any errors or omissions. This book is not intended as a substitute for medical advice. No liability is assumed for damages that may result from the use of information contained within.

Book and cover design by Jenn Zahrt.
Cover image and illustrations by Laura Tempest Zakroff, unless otherwise noted.

ISBN 978-1-947544-61-1
Printed globally on demand through IngramSpark

First printed by REVELORE PRESS in 2024

REVELORE PRESS
1910 4TH AVE E PMB#141
Olympia, WA 98506
USA

www.revelore.press

Serpents of Circe: A Manual to Magical Resilience

Contents

Introduction ~ 9
 Laura Tempest Zakroff

Invocation of the Dark Goddess ~ 12
 Sawyer Massie

Entering Sacred Space
An Invocation and Meditation ~ 13
 Kerri A. Horine

The Living Democracy Sigil ~ 16
 Laura Tempest Zakroff

Linkages & Materia for Political Workings ~ 17
 Ivo Dominguez Jr.

A Spell of Strength for Those Seeking Justice ~ 20
 Luxa Strata

Safety Pins Protection Magick ~ 23
 Vittorio Benetti

Braiding Spell for a Better World ~ 26
 Claire Christine Sargenti

Serpent Medicine for Personal Alchemy:
A Guided Visualization ~ 28
 Christopher Michael

Circe: Witch and Weaver:
A Knot Spell for Protection ~ 31
 Emiliano Russo

Serpents of Circe

Kindness Revival Sigil ~ 34
   Laura Tempest Zakroff

The Danger of Spiritual Bypassing ~ 35
   Moss Matthey

Circe's Hibiscus Tea: An Enchanting Drink ~ 38
   Sophia Kirke

The Potions of Circe ~ 40
   Phoenix LeFae

Invoking the Gate of Reparation ~ 43
   J.R. Mascaro

Lessons of Circe:
The Island of the Self ~ 47
   Joey Morris

Creatures of Resistance:
Nature's Nonbinary Spirits of Protection ~ 50
   Elyse Welles

An Accessible Nature Connection Practice:
Building Resilience in Social Justice Movements ~ 53
   Julie Nowak

Serpent Stones:
Earth Magic for Protection & Resilience ~ 58
   Michelle Cunningham

The Magic of Reweaving ~ 62
   Shannon Rose Raison

A Reversible Anti-Anxiety Sigil ~ 65
   Kajira Djoumahna

A Manual to Magical Resilience

The Calling of the Snakes ~ 66
    Raven Edgewalker

Dedicating to the Dreadful Circe ~ 68
    Irisanya Moon

Circe: Lessons from the First Lycanthropist ~ 71
    P. Sufenas Virius Lupus

Cloak of the Silver Serpent ~ 75
    Mat Auryn

To Call upon the Family of the Sun ~ 77
    Terrance Gamble

A Spray a Day Keeps the Magic Your Way ~ 80
    Richard Levy

A Petition to Isis ~ 84
    Victoria Raschke

Shifting Perspective Sigil ~ 86
    Laura Tempest Zakroff

Dear Transphobe, Thanks for the $400 ~ 87
    Ron Padrón

Lessons from Queen Nanny:
Solidarity & Mutual Aid ~ 89
    Emma Kathryn

Being Radically Resilient:
A Journey of Identity and Liberation ~ 93
    Sawyer Massie & Adam Black

Serpents of Circe

We Are Nothing Without our Dead ~ 96
    Ron Padrón

Ancestral Spiderweb Ward
A Spell for Resilience ~ 99
    Elhoim Leafar

Using an App to Grow Closer during Times of Adversity ~ 102
    Enfys J. Book

Where Do I Go from Here? ~ 105
    Dave Gaddy,
    The Weathered Wiseman

The Aequitas Sigil ~ 106
    Laura Tempest Zakroff

The Work of Us, In This Moment ~ 107
    Alicia "Jynx" Vervain

ACKNOWLEDGEMENTS ~ 110
CONTRIBUTORS ~ 112
RESOURCES ~ 121

A Manual to Magical Resilience

Introduction

IN THE INTRODUCTION TO THE FIRST VOLUME OF THIS SERIES, *The New Aradia: A Witch's Handbook to Magical Resistance*, I began and ended with the phrase *"These are the times we were made for."* I still believe this idea still rings true but six years later, I feel like adding "and these times are often fucking exhausting."

I am a relentless hopepunk of a Witch, but I too can get tired, frustrated, and depressed. I see what other humans are up to and I simply don't understand how people can be so selfish, cruel, and terrible to each other and to the planet.

But then I look around me and know that so many humans are doing good, working hard to uplift, support, love, create, guide, and empower. I see, know, and feel with all of my being that we must continue on fighting and enacting beneficial change. Part of that fight involves resistance, which has been the focus of the two volumes prior to the one you're reading right now. But the fight forward also requires resilience—doing what we can to be fluid, fortified, strong, and responsive—for ourselves and each other.

If we use the Major Arcana of the Tarot as a framework for the zeitgeist of this time, I believe we are moving from the time of the Tower to the time of the Star. This concept has been a large part of my workings and teaching for the last several years, starting with the Power Sigil and building with that energy. I have also found the symbolism of the serpent reaching towards the Star as an embodied guide for transformation and change, from the earth (body) to the sky (spirit).

There has been a lot of focus on the chaos and destruction that is wrought by the Tower—and it's easy to get swept up in the debris and dread. But as magical practitioners, we also must recognize that what we focus on is what we help bring into being. Yes, it's important to recognize what's going wrong and be careful not to bypass the bad stuff,

Serpents of Circe

but it's just as vital to consider the next step: how do we build a better foundation and future going forward? How do we find motivation and inspiration that acts a beacon for ourselves and others? That is where resilience comes in.

Magical resilience is not about simply treading to keep your head above water or trying to maintain the status quo. Rather, it's about plotting a path to the Star—designing a map of hope, strategy, inspiration, and invigoration. Magical resilience is investing energy in our work to truly support living and thriving. To be magically resilient is to be bolstered by belief and beauty, love and legacy, wisdom and wonder. A way to remember and refocus on what makes life worth living. Recognizing relationships, making art, crafting community—investing in tomorrow. Within this book, you will find many perspectives on engaging in magical resilience that I hope will inspire and fortify you.

I also have some advice of my own for magical practitioners trying to function in what often seems like a dumpster fire of a timeline. It's so easy to get overwhelmed and discouraged because the reality is: we can't solve all the problems. There's just no way and you have to make peace with that fact. But there are ways to help solve SOME of those problems. My suggestion is to pick three things to focus on:

1. A personal goal/change/need that affects you at the personal level.

2. A goal or change for your local community that you can directly affect/impact.

3. A goal/hope for society at large type of problem/crisis—whether that's in your state, country, area, world, etc.

Look to how you can make an impact or change at each tier. What magical *and* mundane work is needed that you can do yourself in whatever way is accessible to you? On the days where you feel overwhelmed, go back to the personal. What can you do *today* to help you? When you

A Manual to Magical Resilience

are able to see and affect change at points 1 and 2, it fortifies us and helps to weave a little more difference into the world.

You get to choose what goals have meaning for you. There are no goals that are too small or not enough, as long as they help to sustain and revitalize *your* path and ripple outward. From restorative justice and environmental protection to supporting the arts and sharing our myriad talents—all are vital, necessary, and worthy. What you build for today creates for the next day, the next year, and the next generation.

Don't try to track progress linearly, but instead embrace the serpentine path. You are allowed to spiral inward *and* strike out as needed, to shed your skin to renew your spirit, and begin again with every motion. The microcosm unfolding the macrocosm, one scale at a time. Reach up toward the Star with the whole of you and feel its light within your bones, illuminating you from the inside out.

Your work is necessary and needed. You are needed. Remember, these are the times that you were made for. And together we are shaping them one day at a time—with radical acts of love, magic, and wonder. May the Star upon your brow guide the way.

–Laura Tempest Zakroff
Providence, RI
July 2024

Serpents of Circe

Invocation of the Dark Goddess

Sawyer Massie

Boundless Progenitor of Eternal Darkness,
I hear your soundless screams, terrifying and ecstatic, echoing in the stillness before, between, and after all things.
Stir within my spirit and wake the mysteries of the nothing and everything that is your totality.
Reveal to me your siren song.

Liberated Whore and Veiled Visionary,
I feel the ebb and flow that is your dance ripple throughout the underpinnings of existence.
Release inhibition and teach me your movements.
Make my body a living temple to perpetual experience and transformation, a bathhouse of passion realized and desire fulfilled.
Let me revel in the wonders of the little death.

Unbridled Mistress of Revolution and Evolution,
I see the divine spark that is your torch, smell the scorch and obliteration that is your fury, and savor the richness in the victories of your bloodied and hard-won path.
Enforce within me an integrity that refuses to accept complacency and stagnation.
Walk with me down your crooked, forked path.

Fearsome and Fearsomely Loving,
Awe-Inspiring and Awful,
Blissful and Blighting,
Dark Mother, I conjure you!

She That Is, I conjure you!
She That Was, I conjure you!
She That Will Always be, I conjure you!

A Manual to Magical Resilience

Entering Sacred Space
AN INVOCATION AND MEDITATION

Kerri A. Horine

As WE NAVIGATE THESE TURBULENT TIMES, we can craft our practice based on inspiration from the journey of Odysseus. In times of political division, racial aggression, wars, economic disparity, and general hopelessness, we can contemplate not only the need for shelter but the spiritual act of taking refuge in a sacred space. If we look to Homer for inspiration, we will notice the emphasis on *holy* and *sacred*. Circe's house is holy; the goddess lives within a sacred dwelling in a sacred grove.

It is worth remembering that *sacred* is not synonymous with *safe*. Can we find shelter in the sacred then? Although Circe has dangerous powers, the essence of her power is knowledge. She knows the plants to turn men into animals, but if we look deeper into Book X of *The Odyssey*, we find her advising Odysseus on the need for rest and the absence of joy (460–66). They take refuge in her home, which restores them to health and vitality in many ways. Odysseus and his men are not trapped; he approaches Circe when it is time to depart. He "touched her knees," as the poem relates, "in supplication and the goddess listened" (480–81). She advises him on how to journey to Hades to meet with Tiresias; in fact, she provides him with what he needs. We can approach sacred space with respect, take shelter there, and return to the world with what we have understood and received.

The following practice consists of several parts: contemplation, offering, invocation, meditation, and dedication. To begin, we can briefly consider our motivation. Why are we seeking shelter? What knowledge, insight, or even wisdom do we hope to gain? We can imagine ourselves reaching the doors to the sacred dwelling. What do we bring to offer to Circe? We can make physical offerings such as honey or wine; we can also make mental offerings (or imagined offerings if we have a strong visualization ability). Then we can continue with an invocation. Write your own, use an ancient text, or modify the invocation below as suits your intention.

INVOCATION TO CIRCE

We have had too much wandering,
too little joy.

We are drowned
in the oceans;
our flailing limbs
stir the waves.

Circe, what is the loss?

You are the braided hair glinting
in the sun,
the pattern blossoming
on the loom.

Circe, what is the sacred?

We have arrived at your glade
where the animals cluster,
their barks ringing out as
heat dissipates into shadow.

We light our new fire
in the old storms,
the thick smoke unfurling
rising to the clouds.

A Manual to Magical Resilience

You are slipping past.
Circe, what is the riddle?

You are the voice chanting
in the grove,
the leaves whistling in the
wind's breath.

We are breathing the songs.

You are untying the knots.
Circe, what is the silence?

The meditation will focus attention on whatever feeling or impression arises from the invocation. Notice your breath as if you are breathing in the songs that Circe sings as she works her loom. Try not to cling to thoughts or worry about them when they do rise in your mind. Just let thoughts and worries dissipate. Be receptive in the sacred space of your meditation.

At the end of the session bring your awareness back into the room. Give thanks in whatever way you feel comfortable. Make more offerings if you wish and dedicate for those who are suffering in this time.

Creating and entering sacred space involves respect and caution, but it is important for several reasons. We can gain perspective when we take time out from the ordinary, mundane world and its relentless problems. Not only do we find rest, but we can receive help and guidance. Our relationship with the numinous re-enchants the world for us. If we feel a connection to Circe, it is important to foster that relationship. These relationships sustain us in arduous times. Art, music, poetry—the powers of creativity—connect us to the sacred and uplift us in a world of painful transition.

The Living Democracy Sigil

Laura Tempest Zakroff

BUILT INTO THIS SIGIL:

- Protection & Keeping the Peace
- Justice, Fairness, Accountability
- Freedom, Light to/of Liberty, Illumination
- Truth Revealed, Perspective to see it clearly and wholly
- Healing & Resilience
- Integrity throughout
- CommUnity, Collaboration
- Promote Respect & Equality
- Future-focused, Possibilities, Potential, Hope, Prosper

WHAT TO DO WITH THIS SIGIL: To live democracy is to understand that it's not perfect and that it takes hard work to grow and maintain it. We all must participate in the process to make it function, so this sigil helps to amplify that effort. You can use it as a community focus in virtual or in-person ritual, place on a blue candle (white will work as well), make a place for it on your altar. You may also use this sigil in protection and justice oriented spellcraft as well as when working with deities such as Columbia, Athena, and similar deities and spirits.

A Manual to Magical Resilience

Linkages & Materia for Political Workings
Ivo Dominguez Jr.

IT IS PROBABLE THAT MANY READERS OF THIS ANTHOLOGY have written and enacted a variety of workings that used resonant links, personal concerns, taglocks, and such in spell work. It is just as valuable when you are working political magick to have resonant linkages, but it is necessary to expand your ideas of what constitutes useful linkages and materia to connect to your working's target. Although you may be tempted to focus on individuals, political magick is often more effective when it is directed at structures, processes, organizations, assemblages of people with a particular mission, and the group minds associated with them. Be creative and look at what constitutes a connection when it is a collective or an institution. The following are examples of collective resonant links for workings.

PHYSICAL LINKAGES

If there are physical locations such as buildings, courtyards, green spaces, etc. associated, occupied, or owned by the collective you are trying to influence or target, then there are many sources for linkages. It is not hard to get a bit of soil or a pebble, a vial of water from a fountain or pool, chips of paint, a piece of bark from an old tree that are from the location you've selected. If there is renovation, road work of something similar that opens up other possibilities for materia and how you collect it. There are also options if you are not collecting the material yourself. Sometimes pieces of buildings are removed on renovations and turned into commemorative gifts. For example, the US Capitol visitors center website (https://shop.visitthecapitol.gov/store/collectibles/historic-repurposed-building-materials/) sells paperweights made from sandstone that was in the East front of the building.

Serpents of Circe

Official correspondence is also a great source for a linkage. I have often written letters to politicians, parties, agencies, and various governmental bodies and received responses. These responses are on official stationary and even if they are form letters they are still connected to your target. You are collecting a magickal paper trail. If you are worried about being noticed, pick a fairly innocuous topic for your enquiry letter. Some locations will also have pamphlets, tourist guides, maps, posters, and other publications that can act as linkages as well. While not as effective as materia from your chosen location, paper goods made by or on behalf of the target still work.

You can also create a two part resonant link where you leave or deposit at the intended location to act as a guiding beacon for your working. This is especially valuable if you cannot obtain direct physical linkages. It is important to pick a material that will be easy to hide and will not arouse concern or suspicion. For example, take a small branch or wooden dowel and consecrate it as a wand for the purpose of your working. Whittle off some shavings while pouring in energy and the directive that each shaving is still energetically connected to the wand. Then drop off the shavings at the location or its grounds, ideally in several spots. Go home and use the wand in your working knowing that it reaches directly to your target. Another option is to create a sigil for your working and draw it on two small pieces of paper. Consecrate and energize both sheets of paper at once. One stays intact on your altar and the other is cut into small pieces. Once again, as you cut make sure the pieces remain energetically connected to their twin. Fold up the small pieces and they can be tucked into a variety of places at your target.

SYMBOLIC LINKAGES

The following sorts of linkages rely more on symbolic connection instead of a physical one. The official seals, crests, logos, and flags of collectives can be used as a connection because they are in effect a visual form of their name. These are readily obtained with a quick online search and made tangible by access to a printer. Many organizations and governmental bodies have mission statements, statements of rights or principles, codes of ethics, oaths of office, and so on. These sorts of documents can be read as part of workings to call them to task for broken or ignored oaths and promises.

Most collectives and organizations have a birthdate and sometimes you can find a birth time from the documents that created them. You can create birth charts for them and birth charts are a symbolic representation of their energy. If you don't have the birth time use noon as the time for this purpose.

Materials created for campaigns (candidates, parties, and issues) are mostly symbolic linkages with the faint physical component depending on the circumstances. Signs, buttons, bumperstickers, etc. are all useful though you may wish to warm them up a bit with energy and intention to connect them to their origins. In this case an assortment of campaign materials is more effective than a single piece.

Photos have long been used as linkages, but now we often have access to audio and video recordings that can be used as well. Let's say there is a particularly egregious commercial that is being aired or a noxious speech at a rally. You may consider a working where the offending clip is played at low volume while you drown out the sound by the power of your voice and others if it is a group working. Another possibility is to loudly correct the untruths in the clip and use it as a resonant link to those who have heard or seen it online or over the air.

IS IT A USEFUL LINKAGE?

If you think something may work ask the following to test your idea: ¶ Is it evocative of the intended target? ¶ Is it an analogy that corresponds to the impact of the target's actions? ¶ Is it a metaphor that offers a poetic summary? ¶ Is it a well established symbol for the target?

There are so many possibilities and hopefully this gives you a start.

Serpents of Circe

A Spell of Strength for Those Seeking Justice

Luxa Strata

THIS WORKING IS INTENDED TO PROVIDE STRENGTH and protection to those who are digging in for the long haul in seeking justice. The word justice implies that some injustice or wrong has been committed. When something is justified, it can mean that it is brought back into alignment with something else, some imbalance has been created and then corrected. We can magically utilize the tension that an injustice or imbalance creates towards correcting that imbalance. Nature, afterall, always seeks an equilibrium. Magic and its effects, being properties of the world, can mirror much of what we observe elsewhere in it. I wrote the included psalm for Hekate, who I work with closely and who is well suited for work of this type. She also has a reputation for showing up when She is asked to, and is a reliable ally if treated with respect.

This simple but powerful spell can be performed once, three days in a row, or 9 days in a row; depending on the complexity of the situation or how powerful you would like the spell to be. I perform it at sundown, but use your own discretion. If you chose a multiple day option, you may wish to use a 3 or 9 day candle, keeping it lit for the duration of the spell. You may choose to dress the candle as you see fit, or simply leave it as is.

ᗏ MATERIALS:

Candle & matches, lighter, or other flame source

Psalm 595A

Magical Journal

A Manual to Magical Resilience

STEPS:

In a dim room or other low-light area, recite Psalm 595A while holding whatever you will light the candle with in your dominant hand.

When finished, light the candle and shut your eyes (please be safe), allowing the light of the flame to shine through your closed eyelids. I sometimes receive valuable flashes of insight at this point, so I keep my journal at the ready.

Express gratitude as you see fit to close.

PSALM 595A:

[1] I call upon the Lady as Praxidice,
Hear this, the prayer of your servant.
Come quickly to me, Mistress;
[2] May my words be as honey and oil
That they might be quick and subtle,
Flavored by my gratitude.
[3] Striding across the Heavens,
Over Land and through churning Seas.
You are the Fulcrum
Upon which the levers of Magic turn,
The Axis of the Wheel of the Cosmos.
[4] Queen of Night,
There are no medicines or toxins you do not wield,
No secrets elude your seekers,
No mysteries repel your supplicants.
[5] Give unto me then, Mother,
The power of the Poison which Heals
So that I might extract strength
From past pain and injury.

Serpents of Circe

⁶I honor the fear,
It is my teacher.
I will face my fear.
I will walk into my fear with gladness,
And greet it as a friend.
For the greater my ear,
The greater will be my courage
As I break its bonds.
⁷Mistress, You have opened the Ways
To my wanderings,
I am Holder of the Keys to All Aesthetics,
And the Whole Potential of the Void
By your Grace.
⁸As I emerge once more
From this season of Darkness
Clutching my underworld's prize,
I am binding my breasts
In preparation for battle.
⁹My child is a blade of flame,
My heart is Name,
And I am girded
By your Sacred Light.

NOTE:

I'd like to acknowledge what an inspiration the work of Dr. Cyndi Brannen has been in how I've contextualized some of my experiences working with Hekate. A nod also to Frank Herbert, as Psalm 595A contains my own version of a litany against fear. Should you feel inspired to do so, I encourage you to someday write your own psalms or devotional poems to whom or whatever you choose. I've found the practice to be quite rewarding. Stay strong, stay curious, and remember to Resist!

A Manual to Magical Resilience

Safety Pins Protection Magick

Vittorio Benetti

IN MANY PROTESTS, MARCHES, AND CONFRONTATIONS I have participated in over the years, the need to return home safely after each event was strong. I cannot count how many times I have had the taste of tear gas in my mouth, nor the number of times I have had to run away from police attacks. I saw many protesters arrested and others beaten. At that time, I would need a good, portable magical shield or a protective spell, but till then, witchcraft was only a curiosity for me.

The word *protection* evokes safety, shelter, and inviolability. From my training as a witch and martial artist, I learned that protection is an attitude, a sum of many small precautions and attentions that work together, just like tiles connected to building armor.

Protection spells, symbols, amulets, and talismans have always intrigued me. While studying witchcraft within my tradition, I began researching and collecting these elements from various sources and traditions, focusing on traditional Italian witchcraft. A common trait I found in various traditions, especially in Italian, is using sharp objects, such as blades, nails, needles, thorns, and pins, in protection-oriented magick. Blades like the athame direct the energy, while nails, needles, thorns, and pins dispel and destroy malevolous energy inside the witch's bottle. Again, nails and pins pierce objects, puppets, or lemons in binding spells to fix or bind the energy.

All these pieces of hardware come from everyday household objects. They are very working-class forms of magic. Blades come from the kitchen, nails from carpentry or masonry, pins and needles from tailoring, while thorns or spiky fruits like the witch's burr come from the garden. They are all common yet powerful items.

Thinking about which of those elements brings in an urban guerrilla scenario like a protest scene, where you must run and defend

Serpents of Circe

yourself, I would avoid dangerous objects or things that could fall from your pockets.

My idea of a protest is always peaceful, so the first items I exclude are blades and knives. Even an athame with dull blades could be perceived as a threat and send the wrong message to those around you, especially the police. Regardless of where you live, police officers who believe someone is armed will likely neutralize the perceived threat. Nails and thorns are more portable but still easy to lose and difficult to carry. The last option is needles and pins.

When I hear the word "pin," my mind automatically goes to the punk and skin subculture, a tradition I know very well from my youth when I was part of it. I remember jackets adorned with pins from band merchandise and safety pins used on clothes or as piercings, all in perfect '77 punk style. That underground movement and Italian folk magic share a love for safety pins.

In Italy, grandmothers like mine used to carry extra safety pins in their purses to repair tears in their dresses or fix their veils. However, I later understood that safety pins are also a common and powerful protective object against the evil eye in different traditions. Some families give them as gifts to newborn babies as a good luck charm.

My intuition is to cleanse and charge a pin with protective magick, making it a portable amulet. It could be either a round logo pin or a safety pin.

To maximize the power of the amulet, for the round logo pin, I would create a protective sigil, drawing or printing it on a sticker and put it over the logo side (or in the back of the button if you care about the band logo or want to be discreet).

For the safety pins, I would buy protective charms with symbols of protection and put them on the stem of the pin.

Some examples of symbols could be a pentacle, the eye of Horus, or a walknut for general protection and a cornicello, manofica, or manocornuta against evil eye from the Italian tradition.

A Manual to Magical Resilience

The next step is to cleanse the pin. I would use incense since other methods, like a specific wash, could corrode or rust the pins.

For the incense, I choose spontaneous herbs that can be easily harvested or found in the kitchen, such as:

- Basil
- Lavender
- Thyme
- Bay
- Rosemary

Grind the herbs and create an incense to lit on a charcoal disk.
Choose the right time for your ritual.

For solid protection, I would choose a Tuesday night during Mars hours on a waxing Moon. Tuesday is associated with Mars, the planet and God of protection and defense, making it an ideal time for charging protective amulets.

Open a sacred space and cleanse yourself with smoke. ¶ Call upon your allied spirits or deities. ¶ For this small ritual, we could work with Goddess Aradia from Leland's "Gospel of the Witches" to infuse her rebellious influence or any defensive deity for a more general protection-focused energy. ¶ Pass the pins over the smoke, saying, "With the help of my allies, I cleanse this pin and consecrate it as vessels for protection energy." ¶ Hold the pin in your hands, close your eyes, and visualize an energy shield coming from the pin surrounding you. ¶ Let your energy flow into the object, carrying this intention, and say, "In front of my allies, I charge this object as a protection tool." ¶ Feel the energy flow through you and the pin. ¶ When all the energy will settle down, thank and release your allies. ¶ Close your ritual space.

Now, you are ready to wear your discreet protection shield.

Braiding Spell for a Better World
Claire Christine Sargenti

CIRCE WAS THE FIRST WITCH IN GREEK MYTHOLOGY and a gifted herbalist. She was often found braiding, a task associated with the weaving of the Fates. Robin Wall Kimmer, in her book *Braiding Sweetgrass* tells us "sweetgrass, as the hair of Mother Earth, is traditionally braided to show loving care for her well-being. Braids, plaited of three strands, are given away as signs of kindness and gratitude." Even the Bible, in Ecclesiastes 4:12 tells us that "a cord of three strands is not easily broken." For this spell, we will be magically braiding our intentions for a healthy and sustainable world into three strands.

▷ WHAT YOU WILL NEED:

Three strands (This can be your hair, magical herbs, or green, yellow and purple cords to represent nature, empowerment, and spiritual guidance)

Incense and matches or lighter

Optional charms and amulets to affix to your braid

Rubber bands, hair ties, or strings to hold your braid in place

▷ SOME MAGICAL HERBS THAT YOU MAY WANT TO INCLUDE:

Holy Basil: inner peace, adaptability, spiritual protection

Hyssop: purification and forgiveness

Linden: letting go of anger, calms the heart and soul

Lovage: encourages confidence when taking action

Lavender: cultivates peace and tranquility

A Manual to Magical Resilience

Rose: Opens the heart to love, cultivates healthy boundaries

Rosemary: mental clarity, remembering the old ways

Sweetgrass: promotes happiness, harmony and kindness

Light your incense and cast your sacred circle while using any protection rituals that are appropriate to your lineage. Call in any ancestors, spirit guides or deities that you wish to include in this working.

Hold the materials that you will be using in your hands, and thank them for bringing their unique qualities to your working. Bless your materials with the incense smoke. If you are using three strands, affix them together by tying them in a knot or wrapping them with a rubber band or string. As you begin to braid, meditate on your intentions for creating a better world, filled with healing and love for all living beings and Mother Earth. Transmute your intentions into the braid, knowing that as you weave your strands, you are also weaving the cords of fate. You may wish to turn your intentions into words and pray over your strands as you braid, or use a pre-existing prayer that has been used for generations upon generations. (Some beautiful prayers for the environment, hailing from different traditions around the world include the Haudenosaunee "Thanksgiving Address," the Hindu "Lokah Samastah," Saint Francis of Assisi's "The Canticle of the Creatures," and the Ifa "Oriki Osanyin" among many others.)

Affix any charms or talismans to your braid, and when you have finished, seal your braid with band or string and the accompanying words "so mote it be." Bless your braid with the incense smoke and thank it for participating in your magical working. Extend a prayer of gratitude to your ancestors, spirit guides and deities for their presence in this ritual and bid them farewell. Close your sacred circle, and carry your braid with you as a token of your commitment to create a more sustainable and caring world.

Serpents of Circe

Serpent Medicine for Personal Alchemy
A GUIDED VISUALIZATION

Christopher Michael

Note: While setting the space/intention for the following guided visualization can help establish a container for your experience, it may reveal suppressed emotions, memories, traumas, etc. for which you were not consciously prepared. Please read through the entire visualization before attempting it. If you have concerns about your ability to process, consider using this visualization in trusted company or otherwise have support prepared for yourself.

CLOSE YOUR EYES AND TAKE A FEW SLOW, DEEP BREATHS. Inhale through your nose, briefly hold, and exhale through your mouth. Imagine that you are at the edge of a clearing in a dense forest, with an air of stillness and peace. Take a moment to note the kinds of trees and plants you see, any animal life, and/or colors that may be prominent in the landscape. In the center of the clearing, you notice the figure of a woman and take a few steps closer. She calls you by name, as if she were expecting you. Her voice sounds warm and nurturing; you are comforted by it and begin to approach her. As you draw closer, you sense something ethereal about this woman. Take note of how she appears to you, such as any colors or adornments she is wearing, as well as anything your other senses may gather. Did she happen to share her name with you? As you approach her, she greets you with a tender embrace and you feel a sense of love and belonging. Pay attention to any other emotions that arise when in the arms of this woman.

Freeing you from her embrace, the woman shares with you that she has some medicine to share with you, in the form of her serpent companion. You see a snake with shimmering emerald green scales slither from behind the woman over her right shoulder and down her

A Manual to Magical Resilience

arm. She explains that as her serpent is well-acquainted with shedding old skin, she can help you transform. If your heart is open to her medicine, she will aid in your ability to separate yourself from old beliefs, behaviors, relationships, etc. and step into the new existence you desire.

You take a deep breath as you prepare to receive the serpent's medicine. The woman holds both of your hands as her green snake makes its way from her right arm to your left hand, slithering up your left arm. You feel safe as you are graced by the snake's bright emerald scales, and you sense her willingness to support you with her medicine. She makes her way up to your left shoulder and down to the center of your chest, where she rests her head. As she does, you feel a hum in your heart chakra, and it seemingly begins to open, as if it were a portal.

Shadows begin to emerge from your heart chakra as you feel a heaviness begin to rise within you. The serpent asks you to give her your pain; what ails you so? What has been difficult to bear? What, perhaps, have you been holding onto, attempting to manage on your own? She reminds you that you are safe with her and that she is capable of alleviating even the deepest of wounds that you wish to address. Take some time to feel what's coming up for you. Allow these emotions to move through and out of your body via your heart chakra, with the power of the serpent's medicine.

When you are ready and begin to feel more centered, the snake asks you to take several slow, deep breaths. If you can, allow your exhalation to be slightly longer than your inhalation. You feel a warmth enter your heart chakra, and notice that the shadows have been replaced by a bright, green light with threads of gold. You begin to feel relief, joy, and love where there was once despair. Take note of any affirmations you hear from the woman or her serpent at this time. What other feelings are stirring inside of you? Allow these emotions to expand and feel them at their full capacity.

Take another deep breath as you feel an overwhelming sense of gratitude for this serpent's medicine and the woman who shared it with you. The snake begins to make its way across your chest to your right shoulder, down your right arm, and over to the woman's left arm. You feel as if burdens have been lifted, and rather than just feeling light, you feel empowered. The woman embraces you once more. This time, as her heart chakra makes contact with yours, you feel a bridge between them. She tells you that she and her serpent are here in this space with this medicine for you any time you feel you are in need of it. The woman also reminds you that freeing yourself allows you to aid in the liberation of the collective, and asks that you share this medicine with anyone you feel may be open to receiving it. Take a few deep breaths as you begin to make your way out of the clearing, through the forest, and back into your body.

A Manual to Magical Resilience

Circe: Witch and Weaver
A KNOT SPELL FOR PROTECTION

Emiliano Russo

SINCE THE DAY WHEN WOMEN WERE STILL GODDESSES the shuttle and spool were their tools for changing destiny. Proof of Circe's mastery of weavecraft is found in her Greek name, *Kírke*, which according to Proclus means "shuttle," like that which guides the weft. Homer presents her in Book X of his *Odyssey*, "singing in her beautiful voice as she went to and fro at her great and everlasting loom, on which she was weaving one of those delicate, graceful and dazzling fabrics that goddesses make."

Song, always an integral part of weavecraft, and chanting are sure ways of raising energy and holding intention steady throughout the magical process. As witches well know, singing is weaving with the voice and words are spells preserving intact the primordial power of sound to create. Circe's beautiful voice, a Siren's song that bewitches, reveals her as a theophanic manifestation even before she comes into the mariners' view.

Odysseus' fate, entwined with hers by the song, remains with Circe a whole year. Their son, Telegonus, born after his departure, will be the one to end his life. Though not mentioned in Homer, Eugammon of Cyrene tells the tale of an adolescent Telegonus who journeys in search of his father. Circe arms her son with a spear mounted with a stingray's lethal barb to defend himself from danger. A forced landing on Ithaca after a storm, cattle stolen for survival, the boy comes face to face with the owner defending his property, his father. In a tussle against the thief Odysseus is touched by the poison spear and dies, recognizing his son while breathing his last. The youth desperate over his error takes Odysseus back to be interred on Circe's island. This intricate family affair, seemingly maneuvered and warped by Circe, makes the sorceress a "fatal" Moira capable of cutting the threads of others' lives, thanks to her skill in plotting and warping with deception. It is no accident that one of her epithets is *dolóessa*, identifying her as a queen of deceit, capable of weaving inextricable knots. Precisely, Circe is a profound connoisseur of the ancient Knot Magic.

In Book VIII in a few verses that go almost unnoticed, Homer introduces us to a real magical knot, and he does so when Arete, queen of the Phaeacians, gives Odysseus, before his final voyage to Ithaca, a chest full of treasures, begging him to tie it securely with a knot. What Odysseus performs is a magical knot that Circe taught him many years earlier. Circe's knot is not just any knot; it is a witch's knot. Homer calls it *desmòs*, to indicate its solidity, and it is *poikílos*, "complex," impossible to untie.

This knowledge has brought me to work with Circe in my knot spells, especially when it comes to protection. This is my rewrite of the famous "nine-knot spell." In this version the spell can be used to block an enemy, an unpleasant situation, or a magical attack. I like to cast this type of spell on nights of the new moon to take advantage of the increasing power of the waxing moon. A basic version requires a 13" cord (black ribbon, string, yarn—you choose) and an essential oil of any banishing herb. Being an Italian witch my favorite is rue which can be found in abundance on Mount Circeo, where Circe herself is said to have lived and is only half an hour from home (lucky me!). Perform all your habitual preliminaries. Having done so, take the cord, connect with Circe. Hold the cord firmly, visualize the situation you want to block stating the intent aloud. Begin to knot the cord. I like to knot the extremes, place the third in the center and alternate until all 9 are made. As you knot recite the following:

By knot of one, in Circe's name this spell's begun.

By knot of two, within this cord Circe's power flows through and through.

A Manual to Magical Resilience

By knot of three, mighty Circe hear my plea and with your magic, protect me.

By knot of four, whoever seeks me harm by Circe's witchery will be sore.

By knot of five, wise Circe, bind my enemy and block this strife.

By knot of six, by Circe's will, this spell is fixed.

By knot of seven, Circe's might rises and my sovereignty leavens.

By knot of eight, weaving with Circe we change the Fate.

By knot of nine, Circe, sorceress divine, I claim your witchery, making it mine.

Once all the knots have been made, anoint them one by one with the oil, repeating the incantation on each knot once more. Finally holding the cord in your hands at heart level, say the incantation a third and final time and blow your breath on it to infuse it with life. Keep the cord with you for an entire lunar cycle, returning to anoint it and repeat the spell nine more times during the month, until the next new moon. At this point, for the nine days to follow untie the knots one by one, repenting the spell tied to each knot. When the cord is completely untied, bury it far from home.

May Circe's magic protect you and make you wiser, more powerful and resilient witches every day!

Kindness Revival Sigil

Laura Tempest Zakroff

BUILT INTO THIS SIGIL:

- compassion, empathy
- healing, protection
- strength, courage
- emergence, release, rebirth
- communal support
- recognition, acceptance, consideration, growth
- new beginnings
- a better understand of kindness and its proliferation

WHAT TO DO WITH THIS SIGIL: This sigil calls upon the need for a rebirth of society and community that is infused with renewed active practice of kindness. Use in meditation and ritual to help facilitate change and foster kindness as a foundation in community works. You can also apply it to a candle—a white, light blue, green, or yellow is recommended.

The Danger of Spiritual Bypassing

Moss Matthey

ONE OF THE GREATEST STRENGTHS OF WITCHCRAFT is that it challenges us to think. It allows us to deepen our self-knowledge, become ever more aware of our emotions, and integrate them into a beautiful whole. When difficult emotions arise, we sit with them and allow them to be. In fact, festivals like Samhain often directly involve confronting heavy emotions like grief.

However, there is a way of thinking that avoids this strength that can creep into pagan spaces. Spiritual bypassing involves using spirituality to literally bypass difficult emotions. It goes even further, often assigning a moral value to emotions, and urging you to avoid the "bad" ones. Sometimes this can grow out of bad experiences with spirituality in the past. Those who have left a rigid belief system may have been taught they need to avoid "bad" emotions, push them down and not dwell on negative thoughts. When they leave, they carry those ideas with them, and find a new belief system that helps them avoid their emotions. But anyone can fall into this trap, regardless of their background.

The truth is that emotions don't have a moral value. They are neither good nor bad, they simply are. All of them make up the beautiful whole that is an individual. Unlearning the idea that emotions are an extension of morality is an important step on the journey of witchcraft and claiming your power.

This is easily demonstrated when we think about anger. It is easy to label anger a "bad" emotion. However, if you do so, if you push it down and refuse to work through it or confront the situation that inspired it, you lose an opportunity for personal growth. Saying you forgive someone just because you feel you have to, without doing the work to get there, or seeing meaningful change, will only cause further issues down the line. Anger is not a bad thing. In fact, it can be sacred. Anger can change the world (and it can certainly fuel our magic).

I have personally experienced the dangers of spiritual bypassing. I was raised in a high-control Christian denomination who regularly used spiritual bypassing as part of the control. One very relevant aspect was voting. As "citizens of God's kingdom," voting in elections was forbidden—our vote was already given to God. However, this also meant suppressing all feeling related to politics, and not complaining about the party that happened to be in power. All negative emotions suppressed, no change advocated for, and patiently waiting on God's kingdom was the only acceptable path. By bypassing the natural emotions that arise when injustice is perpetrated by those in power, we were deprived of the opportunity to play any part in change and to be active agents in creating a better world. We were completely deprived of our power.

I also felt the disempowerment of spiritual bypassing in very personal ways. I am a gay man and have been aware of my sexuality since as far back as I can remember. The group I was a part of, however, were deeply homophobic. I was told that God hated people like me, that I could never act on my sinful feelings. Naturally, that led to some very complicated emotions, wrestling with the conflict of my natural feelings while being told how wrong they were. The solution, as usual, was spiritual bypassing. Push the feelings down, push the questions down, and wait on God to "fix" me. I did as I was told, repressed my feelings and the conflict they evoked in me. But that repression came at great cost, manifesting in physical pain that disabled me for years. Spiritual bypassing was far from harmless. Only after I left and accepted myself with my full spectrum of emotions did my pain levels begin to subside. Only once I broke free from the control and sat with my feelings was I empowered to change my circumstances. While pagan groups may not judge sexuality in the same way, the same mechanism is in play when judging emotions like anger or sadness. Assigning a moral value to feelings is a dangerous path.

A Manual to Magical Resilience

The truth is that spiritual bypassing is harmful, especially to minority groups. Think again about the example of anger. If people view anger as morally wrong, then they will never take action to create change. They will bury the emotion; claim they have forgiven their oppressors because it's "the right thing to do." Individuals become trapped in harmful situations because they aren't even allowed to acknowledge them as harmful. Systems of power and oppression are reinforced by this mindset, and meaningful change becomes all but impossible. While telling people they should just forgive and always be "love and light" sounds helpful and harmless, the opposite is true. Love and light will not fix a broken world. You cannot forgive someone into becoming a better person, and no amount of positive vibes will stop your rights and freedoms from being threatened.

Of course, this doesn't mean to be overwhelmed or consumed by our emotions. Again, the great strength of Witchcraft is making space for them all. But it certainly means not allowing anyone to shame you into silence because you're feeling the "wrong" emotions. When something is not right in the world, it is normal to feel that, and only when you feel it are you empowered to help change it. We are complex beings in a complex world, and our magic will always reflect that. Confronting our emotions, making space for them, and taking action when it is needed, is the truly revolutionary path.

Serpents of Circe

Circe's Hibiscus Tea
AN ENCHANTING DRINK

Sophia Kirke

> *Fresh crimson, intermingled. To weep, to smile, the two are indistinguishable.*[1]

CIRCE IS AT WORK WITH HER NYMPHS, in the gardens and wild hillsides of their island, gathering herbs, roots, barks and flowers. They tease each other - "what do you think the next one will become? A wolf? A dove? A lizard? Another pig?" ripples of laughter slide in the breeze, mingled with song, over the lazy surf, turning to sudden sadness. In their hair, they wear large pale and dusky pink, red, purple flowers...they are the picture of beauty and seductiveness—of nostalgia and longing too.

Homer did not paint that scene, nor did Apollonius of Rhodes. It flowed straight from my imagination. There were no hibiscus rosa-siniensis flowers, as far as we know, in the Ancient Mediterranean world. There were close relatives of the hibiscus—a member of the mallow family, and the Greeks called some of the mallow (Malvaceae) 'hibiskos', which gave us the name for that East Asian and Pacific flower.

But hibiscus has a Circean character and so clearly belongs in her island between the worlds. It is beautiful, seductive, slightly hallucinogenic to some people (it can make you high), healing, and delicious. A close Indian relative of the *rosa-siniensis*, the *Hibiscus abelmoschus*, also known as ambrette, produces the most belguiling musky scent, much loved and used in perfumery (and a kind alternative to animal-derived musk).

I have been spending time with the hibiscus plants in the garden, gathering faded flowers, drying them and making tea, a delicious concoction that is both refreshing and healthy. I have to report it has not made me high, but it is delectable in a way I never expected. Above all, I have begun to feel the plant, and especially the flower. Although expressive, it has a quiet, gracious side that reveals itself most in its tea.

MY RECIPE FOR HIBISCUS TEA:

- 2 large handfuls of dry flowers from red or dark pink hibiscus. Try and get hold of some untreated, organic flowers.
- The rind of half a lemon, unwaxed and untreated.
- A tablespoon of fresh ginger root, peeled and sliced.

Place in a large pan and pour hot but not-quite boiling water over all this. Let it cool and steep for 24 hours. Filter through muslin, and warm just enough so that you can add 2–3 dessert spoons of honey (to taste). Let it go cold, then bottle it or put it in a jug, in the fridge, with a dozen mint leaves.

That's it! I drink about three glasses a day in summer. Circe smiles, and winks at me. I have become a butterfly.

NOTE

1. From *Hibiscus*, Li Shangying, Tang dynasty poet, translated by Chloe Garcia Roberts.

The Potions of Circe

Phoenix LeFae

CIRCE UNDERSTOOD THE MAGICK AND MEDICINE of plants. This is not surprising, as witches are often connected to plant medicine and herbalism. However, unlike the local herbalist who may be making tinctures and healing balms, Circe was adding an ingredient that these healers typically didn't. That ingredient is maybe the most important part of the process. That ingredient is magick.

If you want to get super technical a potion is just liquid with some stuff in it—plants, herbs, stones, even animal parts and pieces. A potion could be made for healing, poisoning, or any other desire. A potion could be anything really. A cup of tea at its most basic value is a potion. And yet, a cup of tea isn't a potion because it is the activation of the spell upon the liquid, balm, or solution that turns it into something magickal. That goal or intention doesn't just come in at the last second; when the potion is imbibed. The intention starts when it is decided that a potion needs to be made. The magickal process starts there.

In the stories of Circe, the process of magickal transformation is described in great detail. Circe would create potions ahead of time and then politely serve them to her unsuspecting guests (victims). As these folks imbibed the potion, she then used her wand and spoke magickal incantations in order to activate the magick she placed in the potions.

The fact that Circe used a wand to activate her magick suggests that a potion is simply a mixture of plants, liquids, and other necessary items, but once the wand is used and incantation is said that the mix moves from herbology into the realm of witches. Potentially anyone could make a tincture or healing mixture of herbs, but it takes a witch to turn that into something truly transformative; into a potion.

Circe was/is a very serious witch and magickal practitioner. She is an entity of justice and retribution. She never doubts her power and

A Manual to Magical Resilience

skill. It is important when you take on this working that you remember these things too. It will be important for the success of this potion that you call up your inner power; your inner Circe. You will need to remember that you are an entity of justice and retribution; you are skilled and powerful. You can change your world.

CREATING A POWER POTION

The magickal process of creating a potion starts when you decide to make one. This potion is for power. It is important that you remember that throughout the entire process. As you gather your items, as you purchase a bottle, as you pour water or set up your ritual space, remember that you are a powerful witch. Feel that running through your veins, bones, and cells with each step of creating this potion. Remember your ultimate goal—power. Focus on that, feel that, see it, smell it, taste it.

The Power Potion should be made at a time when you are feeling powerful and you want to bottle up some of that energy. Then it can be used when you need to feel your most powerful. Potions like this do have a shelf life. When the potion is complete it will only last about a week if kept in the refrigerator. However, when the potion is finished fill your jar with half high percentage alcohol and the rest of the bottle with your mixture and it will last up to several months.

It is best if you only use items in this potion that are safe for you to consume. Do not use anything that you are allergic to or not edible.

When creating your Power Potion, you want to feel that energy moving through you; engage with a source of power. Put on music that makes you feel powerful, light incense that adds to the vibe. Imagine Circe in the space with you and see if you can step into her power. Can you feel her energy around you, almost as if you were wearing it like a cloak? Let yourself imagine that you *are* Circe. What she might do? How might she walk, dress, and engage with this process? Fully step into that power.

Serpents of Circe

Once you feel like you are in the right frame of mind, open up the spice cabinet in your kitchen. Pull out all the spices that you have, including salt. Get a cooking pot and fill it with water. Place this on the stove and turn on the heat. Remember you are a powerful creature with each step.

When you feel ready start to add spices into your Power Potion. Open the jars and smell everything. Taste everything. See if what you've got connects you to feelings of power. Trust your instincts and let this process naturally unfold. Don't put in anything that could be irritating (like cayenne pepper) or anything you are allergic to.

Allow the mixture to come to a boil and as it does stir the potion, cackle, chant, tone, and sing over the potion. As your Power Potion bubbles away add in energy by dancing, singing, chanting, stirring, and infusing it with power. If you're uncertain of what to sing or chant, try repeating the word *POWER* over and over again, or say this:

Boil boil toil and trouble
Power build and cauldron bubble
Hold my strength hold my power
Build it higher like a tower

When you feel ready, when your potion is full of power, turn off the heat and allow the potion to cool. As it's cooling continue to sing, dance, and cackle.

Finally, take out your wand (or the first two fingers of your dominant hand) and direct energy into your potion. Recite the above chant, cackle, and dance around like Circe while you send power into the potion. Activate that potion with power.

Put your potion into a jar. Store it in a cool, dry place. Us this potion anytime you need to awaken your inner Circe.

Blessed Be!

Invoking the Gate of Reparation

J.R. Mascaro

IN THE PANEIDOLIST SYSTEM OF MAGIC the concept of just and equitable use of the magician's influence forms a core pillar of our practice philosophy. To that end, the self-initiatic milestones of the work align very closely with the presence of the eighteenth eidolon, a celestial intelligence representing justice, equity, compassion, and fair judgment.

While I strive to draw in and invoke this eidolon mostly for self-actualizing tasks, its power is also used in retributive magic, such as this Gate of Reparation. Gates are energetic patterns anchored to symbolic images through which the practitioners will, aided by an eidolon of aligned purpose, can be manifested into being in a continuous way. A gate is called such because it serves as a literal doorway through which the power of an eidolon can enter our world. The pattern of the gate is the shape which that power takes, drawn so by the magician's will.

The Gate of Reparation, which could also accurately be referred to as The Gate of Recompense, exists as a way to help to right wrongs done to an individual, community, or society, especially wrongs perpetrated by those who twist or exploit systems of justice to do so. Whenever someone acts in the name of justice disingenuously, or outright maliciously, this gate is appropriate to use.

The Eighteenth eidolon is called by the word which ends all injustice, and while that can often be a word of succor to the oppressed it is most definitely a knell of retribution to the cruel and corrupt. As such, this Invocation shouldn't be used frivolously. However, when needed, it can help to set the appropriate wheels in motion.

This gate incorporates symbolism both obvious and subtle. First and foremost, as with all Paneidolist gates, it is contained in a circle. This circle represents the entirety of the causality of this gate existing within the bounds of the magician's will, drawn for a specific effect that will not deviate from its purpose. This circle's edges have been stylized to represent an eroded coin, denoting that the currencies of all empire's are worthless metal to the eyes of the spirits of just judgment.

In the center of the gate we see the boundary of the empty eye, the sigil of the eighteenth eidolon, representing fair and unbiased judgement. Within it, we see an arc of a planar gate, within which is a sun. This sun is inscribed with the ascension loop. These symbols state that, like the sun, the spirits of justice see all, washing over our world like sunlight. This sun shines through the planar gate, implying that the will of this circle spans dimensions. It also shines upon a pyramid, a geometric solid, which represents its ability to alter physical reality. The pyramid is suspended between night and day, symbolic of the existence of this gates will at all moments in time, and in the infinite moment beyond time. The ascension loop reminds us that the inscription of this gate seeks to bring all consciousness toward self realization in compassion and equity.

We have a small scene placed on either side of the planar arc. To the left is a broken pillar in a darkened sky, symbolic of the failures of mortal institutions which have made this gate a necessity. To the right

A Manual to Magical Resilience

we have the sickle of the harvester, suspended in front of the dolmen filed, symbolizing that the unjust must reap what they have sown, and that we must think of what we ourselves have sown and make right our mistakes lest they awaits us in our next iterations.

Toward the bottom of the empty eye we see three arrows, representing the swift execution of justice on all geometric planes of the three dimensional world. Beneath the eye itself, we see a simple scale, in that scale is ciphered the word "æquitas" - denoting that justice should always serve equity.

Finally, at the top of the eye we see a line representation of the intention ascending and surrounding us. A dome of power implied by simple angles.

You may choose to use the gate in this book in your Invocation, or draw your own copy and pin it to an area of your choosing to do its work, or perhaps scribe it on the back of a letter to your elected officials. Your mileage may vary.

The invocation that follows below should be considered a suggestion. If you wish to change the verbiage in a way that more closely aligns with your personal practice, please feel free to do so. I find it beneficial to invoke this gate standing in the sunlight while burning incense, but this is a matter of personal preference.

Before beginning the invocation, engage in whatever centering and ritual space setting exercises you are most comfortable with.

Begin the invocation in a comfortable position, seated or standing to your preference, with the gate pattern either placed on an altar before you or held in front of you so that you may gaze upon it comfortably. Gaze upon the gate and utter the following words:

Grand geometers of the most high, spirits of justice revered by innumerable names throughout the aeons, hear me.

The cruel go forth in your names, though they are blind to your radiance. They serve you not. Their tongues are heavy with lies, their hands are stained with blood, and we can abide them no longer.

May the downtrodden be uplifted.
May the weary know rest.
May the cruel know justice,
So the just may know peace.

A Manual to Magical Resilience

Lessons of Circe
THE ISLAND OF THE SELF
Joey Morris

I HAVE ALWAYS LIVED ON AN ISLAND. It is not the current island on whose shores I find myself, nor is it Aeaea, the fabled island of the Goddess Circe. Yet it has left me contemplating how living on an island is etched into my very bones, as everywhere I have ever lived has been this way, and should the tides change my location again, it will inevitably be another island on which I find myself.

This gets even weirder when examining the etymology of the word, which is from the Proto-Germanic *Awjo (which has Jo within it,) and means "thing on the water." The examination of my surname revealed a similar meaning: "Geis or promise of the Sea."

Water is the universal conduit, without it, life cannot exist. As souls traveling through the human experience, we are created with a large water content and a constant need to replenish and transmute water into ourselves. At any time, we are surrounded by water, and as self-contained souls wandering through life, it is not far-fetched to consider ourselves to be islands, self-contained ecosystems of flesh, bone, water and thought.

The first lesson of Circe is therefore, most certainly, self-mastery. Circe has complete and utter mastery over her island, Aeaea, over the energies that run through its ecosystem, through the plant life, the magick that connects everything, through the beasts that live there, and through every drop of water and grain of sand. It is considered (depending on the storyteller) either her sanctuary or her prison—or both. This could easily be the case for our own bodies and mind. At times we are safest within our own beings. We keep our secrets safe and protected, tucked within our minds, whilst quietly experiencing the world through the lens of our own perspective. We are free to determine, choose, make

Serpents of Circe

our assertions, and replay our own memories. Then there are times where the loneliness of the mind weighs heavy on us, where we are driven to find shared experiences and emotions, and the lack thereof can lead to sentiments of disconnection. Self-mastery is the balance between the two; of celebrating the internal self and the internal realm whilst not isolating to the point where the soul becomes hurt or stagnancy threatens to stilt our emotional growth.

At the same time, we must learn to not give away too much of ourselves to other people. Being protective of the self is reflected within the mythos of Circe; as she turns men into pigs who trespass on her island. This takes on an element of self-preservation when you consider large numbers of men intruding on the island of one lone Goddess in Greek mythology. The tales of the Greeks mention rape in passing so much it almost gets glossed over in their myth. The reality of such heinous acts was trauma and pain, and I for one would not blame Circe for protecting herself with her magical gifts. Self-preservation is certainly one of her lessons.

Another interesting lesson of the self as an island, is to consider what the different elements of Aeaea would represent within ourselves. The beasts that serve as companions and protectors to Circe are particularly fascinating, as spiritual people place particular importance on the energies of animals. Self-knowing and the connections between animals and ourselves is a vast subject. One notion of this comes from psychology, with the animalistic element of the self being the representative of the primitive brain. Personally, I find this need to set ourselves at the top of the ecosystem rather than within it atypical of a mindset which feeds smug superiority and disconnection. Instead, animals represent the parts of us that tap into our wild self, the parts of ourselves which we hide away instead of nurturing, the parts of ourselves that long to howl at the moon and run free. The parts of the human soul which often feel caged by modern society.

Finally, Circe teaches lessons of Transmutation. The self, much like

A Manual to Magical Resilience

the island She inhabits, are vessels of pure magick. We are in a constant cycle of change and flow, able to bring about both acts of destruction or creation, and in most circumstances, of both at once. Our choices are what determine the outcome. We can choose at any given point in our journey. Life can be unforgiving at times but even within the chaos, there is always a form of choice. It is simply listening to the harmonies within the self, our intuition, our inner knowing – that taps into the magic within that enables that choice. In choosing, we begin a process of transmutation; of changing our thoughts, our behaviours, even our circumstances—from one form into another. What an incredible gift that is.

Creatures of Resistance
NATURE'S NONBINARY SPIRITS OF PROTECTION

Elyse Welles

NATURE SPIRITS, THE FAE, THE SPIRITS OF PLACE, nymphs, devas, land spirits... these are terms used to refer to creatures that are one with the land. Tied to the place they live, most nature spirits can't be called on to join you anywhere in the world, unlike deities or spirit guides. But if you're in the place where they reside, they're an unbeatable spiritual ally. And there's no workings they're more allied with than protection magic.

Nature spirits are incomparably powerful. They're often found in sacred places; not just human-assigned places like Stonehenge or temple sites, but at natural sacred places like groves, caves, old-growth forests, or mountain plateaus. These are energies older than human life itself—they have a deep knowledge of chaos and calm, and have experienced things we can't even fathom. This depth and breadth of experience can be tapped into energetically to enhance our magic.

Something powerful about these spirits is that they lie outside of the dichotomous feminine/masculine labels spirits are often given. They are not a part of the fertility-focused spiritual frameworks of some traditional witchcraft practices, and therefore they do not isolate non-cishet practitioners.

When it comes to aid in resistance magic, land spirits are the perfect allies. Like marginalized people who live on the literal margin of society, nature spirits reside in liminal spaces like where a river meets the mountainside, the sea meets the shore, the mossy valleys before a mountain's pass, or crossroads. When you feel you're at the crossroads of human struggles and civil rights, their energy is a powerful grounding force.

I'll add this caveat, though, as a lifelong land spirits practitioner:

A Manual to Magical Resilience

spirits of place and nature aren't concerned with your worries and fears of human-defined success. They don't know what a 401K is, and they don't have the capacity to weigh in on the minutiae of human life.

But they have a shared interest in protection and energetic balance. When humans are in the midst of a period of unrest, the land is shaken by it, too. And when somewhere is less safe because of gun violence, war, destruction, or colonization, especially in threats towards peaceful people made by violent oppressors, the land spirits are fully aware.

The land spirits are on the side of the oppressed. They are looking towards balance and peace, and those on the defensive are usually the ones vying for that. So if you're feeling powerless in struggles of gun violence in the US, in watching the Ukraine War, the slaughter of Palestinians, systematic racial oppression, the fight for equal rights by the LGBTQIA+ community, or other social injustices, tapping into the land around you by calling on the spirits of nature will empower you.

When you invoke nature spirits in your workings, you'll find two things happen. Firstly, you're more grounded. It's literally a grounding practice to connect with spirits of place because they are the essence of the earth itself. You'll also feel more grounded in your life and place in the world because you'll be connecting with the land you live on, and reasserting yourself as a part of the community you're fighting for.

Secondly, their primordial, eternal energy is powerful! You'll feel that energy go towards your cause, and that is a rush to say the least. Their aid and allyship is the beginning of a beautiful relationship. Adding land spirits to your spirit team, for protection magic and grounding of any kind, is a very rewarding experience, especially if you inhabit the liminal spaces of the nonbinary or non-gendered communities, or if, like me, you simply prefer your witchcraft to be less gendered overall.

If you've never worked with land spirits before, bringing offerings to the outdoors, usually of food or drinks safe for the animals of your area to consume, is a great way to introduce yourself. And then, when you've felt their presence or connection and feel comfortable working with them, invite the land spirits as you would a deity in ritual or spellwork. A simple invocation like "energies of the land, spirits of place, I invite you to join me in my working to relieve Palestine of suffering by Israel's attacks, may a ceasefire be imminent. Lend me your powers of grounding and peace to send my energy towards this worthy cause."

Even though the land spirits are only present where they reside, you are transmuting their powerful energy towards the cause you're working in your spell or ritual. In a way they act like an amplifier in spells like this. Let the land spirits empower you to take steps forward in your own activism. With the eternal forces of the land spirits behind you, you'll be unstoppably grounded and empowered.

A Manual to Magical Resilience

An Accessible Nature Connection Practice
BUILDING RESILIENCE IN SOCIAL JUSTICE MOVEMENTS

Julie Nowak

NUMBER OF PEOPLE: This activity can be practiced as either an individual or group.

TIME REQUIRED: you choose! (e.g. 5 minutes, 1 hour, etc)

SETTING: anywhere that is accessible to you (indoors or outdoors)

MATERIALS:

↦ A way to connect with nature (see list of options under Step 1)

↦ Optional: a timer

OVERVIEW:

In this practice, you will choose a location or other accessible format for connecting with nature. Being outdoors is not accessible to many of us, but we can connect with nature anywhere—even while lying in bed!

The purpose of this activity is to carve out time and space to help you feel resourced, so that you and your community can approach social justice work with more resilience. When we feel grounded, we have more capacity to create an equitable world.

Connecting with land is also an important part of challenging colonialism. Many of us live on stolen land, and colonialism keeps us disconnected from both local Indigenous land and from our ancestral lands. Additionally, we as humans are part of nature! Viewing ourselves as separate is a colonial way of thinking. There is a lot of power when we connect with land and the living world through this lens.

Serpents of Circe

HOW TO DO THIS PRACTICE:

The following six steps will help you create a customized practice for connecting with nature that is both accessible and meaningful. If any of the steps are activating, please pause and take care of yourself. You can alter any step to help you create safety. If in a group, present the steps as an invitation, not a requirement.

STEP 1: PLAN YOUR LOCATION AND FORMAT.

Choose a location and format for connecting with nature that is accessible to your body and mind. Some options include:

🐍 OUTDOORS:

A park or forest

Your backyard or balcony

A city tree or plant

🐍 INDOORS:

A window to look out

Nature images or videos (e.g., search on Youtube or Google images)

Nature sounds (e.g., search on Youtube or a podcast app)

House plants

Food in your kitchen (e.g., a whole fruit or vegetable)

Animal companions

Imagination/visualization of being in nature (e.g., in your local area, or where your ancestors are from, or somewhere imaginary, etc.)

If you are doing this practice as a group, you can optionally share a nature format together. For example, you could share a nature video on Zoom. Alternatively, each group participant can choose their own individual format.

STEP 2: REFLECT ON WHAT IT MEANS FOR YOU TO CONNECT WITH NATURE ON INDIGENOUS LAND.

You can do this ahead, if you need more time to research.

Find out who the original Indigenous caretakers are of the land you are on (and/or the location of the nature content you are using, if known).

Make a plan for what actions you will take to support Indigenous sovereignty. This could include donating money, learning more, and educating others.

Here is a website where you can learn about whose land you're on: Native-land.ca

For more info and examples of Indigenous projects to support, check out this anonymous google doc about the #LandBack movement, titled "Turtle Island indigenous reparations and land rematriation support." It is available at this link: tinyurl.com/4u3n9yt5

STEP 3: SET AN INTENTION.

Take some time to write or think about what you want to focus on with this practice. How do you want to feel? Why do you value this practice? How does nature relate to your social justice work?

Here are some examples of statements that you can use or adapt for your intention:

⮕ My intention is to feel grounded and to regulate my nervous system.

⮕ I value taking this time to connect with nature so that I have more resilience to engage in social justice.

⮕ Connecting with land is part of unlearning colonialism.

Serpents of Circe

STEP 4: SPEND YOUR DEDICATED TIME ENGAGING WITH NATURE THROUGH YOUR SENSES.

Set yourself up with whichever format or location you chose in STEP 1. Decide how long you want your practice to be, and you can optionally set a timer.

Begin observing what you experience through your senses, if this feels accessible and safe for you. You can either let your mind wander, or be more intentional with how you observe.

Here are some prompts to help guide you:

- What do you see/hear/smell/taste/feel?

- If your chosen format does not include some of the senses, what do you imagine them to be?

- What colours and shapes stand out to you?

- Where do you observe movement and stillness?

- How many different sounds do you notice? Are they layered?

- Describe what you smell with adjectives. (e.g., earthy, fresh, wet, sweet, floral)

- If you are connecting with a food item, what does it smell or taste like?

- If you are outdoors, open your mouth and describe the taste of the air.

- What textures can you touch or see? What do they feel/look like?

STEP 5: REFLECT ON THE EXPERIENCE.

After you finish the practice, take some time to write or draw or think about your experience. If you are in a group, you can discuss this together.

A Manual to Magical Resilience

Here are some reflection prompts:

🔖 How was that practice for you?

🔖 Which of your senses felt the most engaged?

🔖 If it feels safe to observe your body, notice any physical sensations you feel. Try to observe without judgement.

🔖 Did you have any interesting thoughts or ideas during the practice?

🔖 Review the intention you set at the start of the practice. How did it affect your experience of connecting with nature? How will you carry that intention into other parts of your life?

🔖 Do you have any other takeaways?

STEP 6: SHOW YOURSELF APPRECIATION FOR DOING THIS PRACTICE, AND MOVE ON WITH YOUR DAY.

Thank yourself for carving out this time and space to build resilience and connect with nature.

Now go onwards!

Serpent Stones
EARTH MAGIC FOR PROTECTION & RESILIENCE

Michelle Cunningham

MINERALS HAVE ALWAYS BEEN incorporated into the craft of the wise ones, the cunning folk and witches of history. Sacred fossils and stones included as grave goods in Neolithic and Bronze Age burials attest to their long lineage of spiritual significance—stone magic that was carried across the ages to find record in the writings of Pliny the Elder and medieval lapidary texts, as well as marrying into the folk traditions of countryside dwellers. From these sources common themes have emerged, including the apotropaic or protective virtues of certain fossils and stones, as well as the peculiar association of many of these same mineral materials with the serpent, and serpentine energy.

In many ways this connection is unsurprising. Serpents are representative of the earth element, spending the cold part of the year brumating under stones in dark earthy dens, only to emerge in warmer months with a preference for basking on hot rocks in the midday sun. Snakes and stones are intimately entwined in art and myth, from the serpentine spirals and zig zag motifs etched into the giant megaliths of Northern Europe, to the fabled *ovum anguinum*, the "serpent's egg"—a stone noted by Pliny as sacred to the ancient Druids. In the Greek pantheon, it was Gaia who sent the giant serpent Python to guard the Omphalos stone at Delphi, the great navel of the world. From Python derives the name of Delphi's high priestess and oracle, Pythia, who would receive visions aroused by vapours emanating from rock chasms where the snake's body lay decomposing within the earth.

Serpent energy and stone energy can both be said to be coiled and potent, full of generative force and poised for action, or defence—should it be needed. Snakes and stones stand as protective guardians to chthonic realms and act as magical intermediaries between this and the

A Manual to Magical Resilience

Otherworld. Both are powerful agents of change and renewal in their own right, embodied by the snake's shedding of its old skin and in the transformation of stone on its journey through the rock cycle. In building a toolkit for magical resistance, we can turn to the primal energies of serpent and stone to harness qualities of protection, resilience, justice, and regeneration.

The following are a few "serpent stones" long employed in folk magic traditions. In challenging times, under the cloud of oppression, these sacred stones offer their unique virtues and ancient apotropaios when worn or incorporated into spells and ritual. Revealed in their formation are further energetic clues as to their symbolism and function in magic. Should you not have any of these fossils or stones at hand, look to the land and the rocks around you. Draw upon the serpentine forces that pulse though the geology beneath your feet. Stand your ground, and be filled with the power of earth in all of your workings.

¶ SNAKE STONE

('*Cornu Ammonis*') – FOSSIL AMMONITE

Once thought to be the remains of snakes—petrified and rendered headless by the actions of saints and seers—Ammonites are extinct predators that once ruled primordial seas. Their enigmatic spiralling shells are composed of a series of chambers which were sealed off to help regulate buoyancy and propel the creature through turbulent waters. Ammonites are connected to cycles of time, the necessity of change, and prophetic visions. In folk magic, they were stroked or steeped in water to effect a cure and protect against bodily harm.

Magic & Symbolism: Binding magic, used to cut off energy at the source and "petrify" adversaries, self-regulation and hope in the midst of challenge, progress, creation, dreams and inspiration for the future.

Serpents of Circe

⁋ SERPENT'S TONGUE

('*Glossopetra*') – FOSSIL SHARK TEETH

Now recognised as the fossilized teeth of *Otodus megalodon*, Serpent's Tongues were believed to fall to earth during a lunar eclipse— an event that bestowed them with divinatory properties, control over the tides, and an ability to silence the wind. Dipped into wine or worn as a charm, Serpent's Tongues were popular throughout the Middle Ages as an antidote to poison and a portent of harm. On behalf of their serrated edges, they have also been used to sever malignant energy and sympathetically ward against injury.

Magic & Symbolism: Protection, vitality, cord cutting, turns the tides of a situation and silences the opposition, entices favourable change, bequeaths graceful speech and writing for political activism.

⁋ ADDER STONE

('*Glain Neidr*') – HOLEY STONE

In many regions of the British Isles, Adder Stones or Serpent Beads (also known as Hag Stones) are naturally holed stones often composed of flint, created by the movement of water or the boring action of mollusks. Hung by red thread about the neck or above the door, Adder Stones were used as prophylaxis against snakebite and charms against the evil eye. In folk magic, the hole is regarded as a portal to the Otherworld through which objects and spells may be passed with the intention to bless, banish, or birth into being.

Magic & Symbolism: Banishment, transmutation, manifestation, renewal, protects against malevolent energies, relieves feelings of exhaustion and overwhelm, community healing, rebuilding and rebirth.

¶ SERPENT'S EGG

(*'Ovum Anguinum'*) – FOSSIL ECHINOID

While there is some debate over the geological identity of this mysterious stone—mentioned by Pliny as arising from the secretions of a writhing mass of serpents—many scholars believe the Ovum Anguinum was likely a fossilized sea urchin, or echinoid. Widely employed in folk magic, Serpent's Eggs (also known as Brontia or Fairy Loaves) were used to protect the home from misfortune, as well as to curry favour in lawsuits. Their stellated forms embody the energy of the Star, acting as a guiding light and connection to the great beyond.

Magic & Symbolism: Resilience, justice, success in legal matters, threshold magic, protection from sudden shock and harm, support during times of crisis, safe passage, empowerment, optimism, possibility.

Serpents of Circe

The Magic of Reweaving

Shannon Rose Raison

I ONCE FOUND MYSELF STANDING AT THE INTERSECTION OF TIME: my body was in the present, but my consciousness was thrust deeply into the past—and my desperate desire to experience something different reached towards the future. I struggled to comprehend how something beautiful could be created from what had unravelled around me.

At this place that existed beyond time, I met a wise being who tended a deep well. They shared with me that we weave the threads of what is to come with the threads of what has gone before. That it is through unweaving these threads of the past that our fingers learn the skill necessary to weave the fabric of the future.

This knowledge felt at once restrictive and expansive. Are we really limited to only using the threads of that which has gone before? How then could we ever create change, shift the fabric of reality?

And yet, there before me spread out farther than the eye could see was tapestry upon tapestry. Each uniquely different from the next and all woven of the same thread. Red and gold, central colours to some, took a background seat to purple and green in others. How could so much variability be created from the same materials?

I was shown that it is in the weaving and unweaving. Each time a new pattern is unravelled the weavers' fingers discover another angle or facet, another way to imagine the same material into new and unique forms. Each time a tapestry is rewoven this learning is integrated, expanded upon, expressed in new and different ways.

As I looked at them all spread out before me—as far as time can see and beyond—some appeared similar, parallel, spirals back around to the same place. Some were barely recognizable as the same threads at all. Engulfed in the depth and sheer volume, I realized it was unclear

A Manual to Magical Resilience

where they began and where they ended. An expression of timelessness I could only feel in my being but not truly understand or put in to words washed over me.

We are so deeply visited by the weavings of the past when it is time for us to learn from their unravelling. When we need only the knowledge that specific unravelling can give us to weave anew.

We are at once constrained and emboldened. We work with the threads we are given, but we also have the opportunity to weave them in new and ever-expanding ways.

A Working for Reweaving

This magical working brings us into the conversation of how to work with what we already have. To weave a new culture of liberation and love for all from the threads of our current existence. This description is meant as inspiration—not direct instruction. Make it your own, adapt it to your working, reweave it with your own beauty and magic.

This magic could be big or small. Maybe you are reweaving a personal experience, maybe you are individually or collectively working with a current political event or state of affairs. Whatever your focus, find a used physical object that represents it—old clothing, a trinket from the thrift store, discarded flyers or pamphlets—whatever your magical inspiration directs you towards.

The magic here is in the process—how do you unweave and reweave this physical object? How does the process of doing so support your magic, deepen your understanding of the physical reality it represents?

Take apart this object—cut it, break it, delicately unwind it, use your own magical practice in sacred space and personal guidance as tools to explore how to do this. If you get stuck use it—sit with it, explore it, what information does this give you about the situation? Ask for support—magically, from community, what do you need to dismantle this object in it's current state?

Serpents of Circe

This working may take an hour, days, or years. Trust and learn from your process.

When you are ready—when it is clear it is dismantled—begin the reweaving. What did you learn from deconstructing it that informs how to make it anew? What shape will it take? How will you incorporate all the pieces. Yes, all the pieces. The seemingly broken, the one's that don't fit, the awkward—this is abolitionist magic. There is deep wisdom in weaving in all of the pieces—it may not be easy, but it is the work. What do you need to support yourself in this? To include that which you wish to discard? What is it you wish to discard? What information does this give you?

Use tools and support—your magical practice, your communities both human and other-than. Reweaving does not need to be done alone.

This working is a spell for reweaving something that needs change. Remaking a used item as new, reweaving a liberatory future for all. What wisdom is created from using that which already exists to create something new? What do you learn in the reweaving? How does this magic inform your activism, your role in community, your magic in the broader world?

How are you reweaving our current fabric of reality into a tapestry of love and liberation for all?

A Manual to Magical Resilience

A Reversible Anti-Anxiety Sigil

Kajira Djoumahna

Summary: This sigil is for combating and draining away anxiety of any origin, because less anxiety enables greater resilience. Location and date of creation: Windsor, California, May and June 2023

WHAT ELEMENTS WENT INTO THIS SIGIL:

    Wholeness, protection
    Waxing confidence, reaching (or if reversed, draining of fears)
    Spirit, vigor
    Stability, strength, foundation
    Security
    Calm, easy passage
    Releasing fears

SUGGESTIONS FOR USE: This sigil can be flipped by turning your book so that the bottom becomes the top. Various forms of anxiety may respond more effectively to one orientation, or perhaps both will be helpful in different circumstances or on different days. You can try resizing one or more of the elements around the perimeter to enhance certain parts if you desire. Try drawing it in brown, blue, purple or black. Place in your pillowcase, under car floor mats, and anywhere else you wish.

Serpents of Circe

The Calling of the Snakes

Raven Edgewalker

IN KENT, UK, I AM A YOUNG CHILD, watching a small olive-green grass snake slither through the grasses. My mother tells me stories of her own childhood when grass snakes were so numerous that she and her siblings would collect them and wind them around their arms and necks like jewels. She told me of the adders on the heath, their white zigzags marking them as vipers, poisonous. Shy, and elusive; rare, that they would rather hide than attack.

Come unto us! Shy ones, stealthy ones, beauteous ones! You who slip lithe and silent amongst the grasses. Come to us grass snakes, and teach us to move unseen, show us the hidden paths. Come unto us, sun-worshiping adders, show us when to hide and when to defend ourselves.

In London, I am a teenager, wandering the halls of the Tate, seeking something that I cannot name. My skin feels too tight, I want to rip it from me in ribbons. I see her on the wall, full length, intent, furious, gaze, pouring and pouring bright green poison from her raised bowl into the waters below. She, Circe, that painting, wakes something within me my teenage self, something that begins to transform and uncoil.

Come unto us skin-shedders, remind us how to shed the skins of culture and tradition that constrict and constrain us. Skins that keep us small and separate. Show us how to burst forth, to grow, to act, to speak, to uncoil and to expand into action. Show us how to grow into fierce wise beauty, show us how to create new cultures.

In the desert, a still oh so young adult, I ride an Arab stallion into the desert mountains before dawn to watch the sunrise, turning the

A Manual to Magical Resilience

mountains pink and luminous. I am beginning to understand the path I've chosen is full of twists and turns and challenges. In the bright hot sun on the way back to many-peopled resort I'd escaped from, the guide points out the coils of a desert sand coloured snake on a rock and makes a warning sign with his hands and a shake of his head. My horse skips sideways, and I go no closer.

Come unto us! Snakes of the hot dry lands, where the sun bakes hard the rocks. Rise up and warn us with your forked tongues of the dangers seen and unseen. Guide us, show us the paths best taken, show us the twists and turns and dangers ahead. Uncoil yourselves from your desert rocks and join with us, protect the lands and your peoples, our peoples.

In front of a screen in the UK, I talk to a beloved thousands of miles away in Brazil. We talk of climate change, of rains and droughts, and floods and fires. We talk of fear and hopelessness, and we talk of magic, of rising up, of creating change. We talk of physical and non-physical allies, the beings that inspire and challenge us to do more, to be better, to continue to learn and listen and teach. We talk of family of choice, of allies, expected and unexpected.

Come unto us! Mighty anaconda of the Amazon, powerful ones, world-eaters, world changers! Rise from the muddy waters, guide us with your wisdom, ancient ones, vast ones, serpents of the water depths. Messengers of the gods, carry their words to our ears. Give us the wisdom to act, to change and transform, to bend and not to break. Protect us in the work that our hearts call us to do, protect us so that we might in turn protect and sustain that lands that are home to all.

Mighty Serpents of the world, we call to you, we seek your aid.

So, may it be.

Serpents of Circe

Dedicating to the Dreadful Circe

Irisanya Moon

> *[Circe speaks:] Trust me. If you doubt that and have no faith*
> *in your appearance, then consider me,*
> *a goddess, daughter of the glorious Sun,*
> *who has great power with spells and potions,*
> *and yet **I promise to be yours**. So spurn*
> *the one who spurns you, and **reward the one***
> ***who now pursues you**. In that single act*
> *let your revenge repay the two of us.*
> *—Ovid, Metamorphoses, 14.32–36, translated by Ian Johnston*

ACCORDING TO SOME STORIES, CIRCE was exiled to the island of Aeaea as punishment for how she chose to use her magick, sending this powerful being far away from society. If She were sent away, She wouldn't cause more "trouble."

The world is a sorcerer too, trying (and often succeeding) in conjuring visions of isolation, apathy, and overwhelm. Through oppression, capitalism, patriarchy, and more, the powers that be cast spells of disconnection. They seek to send everyone to their own islands, alone and frustrated.

But you are not alone.

Circe can be an inspiration, a co-conspirator, and a more-than-willing accomplice.

Circe does not hesitate. She knows what to do, how to do it, and when to step in. She is a lover, and She loves, She is a healer and a hexer. She is a force to be reckoned with, one with spells and potions that will remind you of who you are.

Circe can look at you with Her golden eyes and remind you of the magick inside you. This fair-locked goddess will show you how to recog-

A Manual to Magical Resilience

nize the power in yourself. How to act on it.

Pursue Her. Call on Her. Dedicate yourself to Her.
She has promised others to be theirs—why not you too?

📎 YOU WILL NEED:

Altar to Circe

An invocation/prayer to Circe—why do you want to dedicate to Her?

Food

Drink / libation

Three herbs that make you feel powerful and wise

A bowl of water

If you can, it would be nice to be outside in nature for this ritual, as though on the island with Circe. But if you cannot, you can also take time to think about what the forest of Aeaea looks like to you in your mind. Close the door to the room you are in and know yourself to be there.

Set up an altar for Circe with images, offerings, and other things you think She'd like. Depending on your preference, you can put this altar in the middle of the ritual space or off to the side.

Begin by creating sacred space. I would include a cleansing, grounding, and circle casting to ensure the best possible container. Take your time. This is not a time to rush into magick.

Once the space feels sacred, call out to Circe with the invocation or prayer you have created. Take your time to make sure She hears not only the words but also the emotions behind those words. Let the words hang in the air briefly before moving on to the next part.

Take the bowl of water and remember it as the spell of connection from that prior chapter. Look at your reflection in that water. See how

Serpents of Circe

you are powerful just as you are and that you are worthy of stepping into more power with Circe as a guide.

Place the herbs you have chosen for power into the water, speaking about each herb as you add it to the water. Stir this around clockwise at least three times. Once the water and herbs are stirred, think about what the water contains and how you have created it. You have chosen this potion based on your intuition and wisdom.

Now, you have a few options: you can choose to disrobe or make a part of your skin more available. You can anoint yourself or bathe yourself in this water and herb mixture. This will help you take in your intention by offering it to your body's largest organ.

You can choose the place where the water goes and how it will be placed there. You might want to focus on your heart, hands, head, etc. This part is up to you. Maybe you want to put the water on the places that align with your intentions. Or maybe you want to put the water on places that feel like they need more power.

Once you have anointed yourself and used up all the water, turn to Circe's altar and ask that She witness you in your dedication. Ask for Her blessing and ask for Her strength. You might commit yourself to a year and a day with the idea you will renew this commitment if it feels right at that time.

Allow yourself to feel the power of Circe on your shoulders, the power of the great enchantress along your skin. This magick is waking up inside you already. You will be working together; let the magick begin in this moment.

Whenever you feel ready to be complete, and there is no rush, take some of the food and drink and offer it to Circe. Then, take some of the food and drink for yourself, allowing yourself to ground down into the magick you have created together.

Once you feel complete, thank Circe for all that She is and all that She might become in your life. Open the circle and clean up.

A Manual to Magical Resilience

Circe: Lessons from the First Lycanthropist

P. Sufenas Virius Lupus

ALTHOUGH ZEUS IS REPORTED IN ANCIENT GREEK ACCOUNTS to be responsible for turning the Arcadian King Lykaon into a wolf, and is thus credited for the origin of werewolves, in reality the earliest such account in the literary history of ancient Greece is from Homer, in the *Odyssey*, and this transformation is attributed to Circe. Though not directly depicted in Homer's epic, the other animals on the island when Odysseus and his sailors arrive include wolves, and later classical literature always includes wolves as among the forms that Circe's sorcery wrought in her victims. These transformations can be understood in many ways: the pig transformations that Circe creates in the sailors may be a reflection of their truer natures as lecherous gluttons; but, what are we to conclude when the forms assumed are, in some ways, more powerful than the merely human?

We must first understand lycanthropes and werewolves—both of which mean the same thing, "wolf-humans" or "human-wolves," but in Greek and Anglo-Saxon respectively, and which match terms from other languages (e.g. Irish *ferchú*, Welsh *gwrgi*, etc.)—not as what Hollywood monster films and television portray them as, but instead as humans that become wolves more fully, not as a senseless human-wolf bipedal hybrid. (For such hybrid beings, usually with humanoid bodies and wolf- or dog-heads, Hekate is your Goddess... as She is if you would prefer cynanthropy or "dog-human" rather than "wolf-human" transformations...but those are other stories!) Further, the vast majority of lycanthropic occurrences in literature have nothing to do with infection via biting, transformation under the Full Moon (in fact, the New Moon is attested earlier!), vulnerability to silver bullets, or anything else commonly featured in the trope's popular examples. Transformation by spell, curse, or other magical means, as with the

Serpents of Circe

case of Circe, is far more the norm than the exception where the werewolf motif is concerned.

Not simply one type of shapeshifting available to shamanistic practitioners or general magical techniques, werewolves represent a unique phenomenon witnessed across many ancient cultures, especially in the Indo-European world, of youthful hunter-warriors closely identified with certain ferocious animals, of which wolves are the most prominent example due to their social organization and cooperative pack tactics. Transformation was not always literal, and could be a metaphorical characterization of their behavior, an identification and re-naming, or even adoption of articles of attire (wolf skins and pelts, or headdresses and masks made from wolf skulls or faces, etc.). They lived outside of social structures, and were often portrayed as outlaws, but were also closer to nature; to this day, the most common term for "wolf" in Modern Irish, *mac tíre*, means "son of the land."

Such youthful (but not always exclusively younger) hunter-warriors provided a first line of defense for their tribal cultures, but also served as spiritual protectors and champions in turning back malevolent supernatural influences as well as physical attackers, and had responsibilities for the health and fertility of their people. They interacted with Deities, fey, and land spirits, interceded with the dead and Ancestors, and could represent any of these spiritual beings when ritually interacting with the living.

Some scholars attempted in previous generations to portray these groups as "men's societies" exclusively, but the evidence's reality demonstrates that women and people of diverse other genders (or who shifted gender!) also participated in such groups equally. Homoerotic relationships were also attested amongst these groups' participants, and most of the ancient myths that feature homoerotic love (e.g. Gilgamesh and Enkidu, David and Jonathan, Achilleus and Patroklos, Cú Chulainn and Fer Diad, and the nymphs of Artemis, etc.) were amongst age grades and warrior classes that partook of the features of lycanthropic warbands.

A Manual to Magical Resilience

There was a mythic dimension to some of these accounts, but a practical and very real dimension to them is also beyond doubt, and such groups of youthful outcasts that were nonetheless essential for the survival of society existed in several civilizations until recent centuries. Certain customs of military services and first-responder organizations, street gangs, youth scouting activities, and a number of other social groups still draw upon the lycanthropic phenomenon for aspects of their symbolism and ritual practice.

Though guerilla-trained and able warriors, and prone to raiding and skirmishing amongst themselves as a means for alleviating adolescent anti-social tendencies, lycanthropic groups were not primarily aggressive, but instead were defensive in their intent and actuality. In calling people to become what they most truly are through her magic, perhaps Circe is summoning individuals today to become such guardians and protectors through her transformations. Individuals will not simply "Be werewolves and do crimes," and in fact should be quite the opposite, instead using their natural talents and developed skills in physical self-defense as well as magical training and psychic gifts to shield those unable to protect themselves, be called upon in emergency situations, and to help defend society-in-general from the material and spiritual ravages of political and social toxicity and the very real threats posed by conspicuous consumption, corporate greed, and Christofascist attempts to control people's bodies and public spaces.

Heeding the call to become such neo-lycanthropes will involve advocating for and defending female bodily autonomy as equally as indigenous land and water rights, LGBTQQPIA2SNB+ civil rights, climate change awareness, and standing against corporate ownership and control, capitalist overreach, and the creeping menace of dominionist seizure of government and dominant religious hegemonizing of legal and judicial institutions. Spiritual protection need not be against monsters and ghosts visiting on a Samhain eve as much as it might be fighting the egregores of "pro-life" and anti-trans activism and their legions of prayer warriors, and meeting these in the trenches of both on-the-street protests as well as ideological and psychic arenas. The potential deployments do not end there.

Circe once transformed impure men into the outward form of beasts they truly were internally. Now, may she transform those called to such protective roles into more empowered guardians that know the best of the wisdom of the animal, divine, and human realms.

Cloak of the Silver Serpent

Mat Auryn

THE INVOCATION OF THE SILVER SERPENT'S CLOAK acts like a quarantine suit for your energy field, ensuring that you do not absorb any negative energies from your surroundings or the people within it. Just as a quarantine suit provides a physical barrier to prevent contamination, the Silver Serpent's Cloak creates a protective energetic shield around you. This shield reflects and repels hostile energies, keeping your spirit and body safeguarded against external negativity. I use this visualization and invocation in the most intense situations, such as protests, highly charged confrontations or extremely haunted locations, where the risk of picking up detrimental energy is at its highest. This practice helps maintain my inner strength and resilience, allowing me to move through challenging environments with protection. Some of the powers of Serpent deal with transformation, protection, and resilience; it will shed discordant energy like old skin and rise pure and anew. The silver coloring of the snake is particularly important in this, as it reemphasizes the properties of not taking on external energies. Typically, silver is associated with protection, purity, and clarity. It protects against unwanted energies, sort of like a mirror, reflecting them away from yourself.

TO PERFORM THIS:

Stand with your feet close together, your arms down at your sides. With your eyes closed, breathe in deeply through your nose, then slowly exhale through your mouth. Imagine a large and powerful shining serpent, curling slowly around and around yourself, with every breath you take. Its silver scales are radiant and reflective, forming a protective barrier that repels negative energies. Affirm to yourself mentally that this serpent's power will shed any energy that isn't yours that will try to attach itself to your field while it is activated.

Now, call upon the serpent's power by reciting the following invocation with intention and focus:

Serpent strong, of ancient lore,
Cloak me in your power's core.
Guard me from the dark and cold,
With scales of silver, brave and bold.
Let no external energies adhere,
Keep my energy safe and clear,
With your strength, I walk the land
Transformed and shielded by your band.

Visualize any negative energy or attachments sliding off you, much like a serpent shedding its old skin. See this negativity dissolving into the ground beneath you where it will be transformed in the Earth, leaving you cleansed and revitalized. Know that it will continue to do this whenever an external energy comes into contact with it, trying to attach to you.

Really embrace the power of resilience as the serpent's energy infuses you. Sense its strength and adaptability becoming part of you, making you more capable of facing any challenge.

Visualize the serpent transforming into a silver cloak of snake scales settling comfortably around you, its energy continuing to shield and empower you. Recite the closing words:

Thank you, Serpent, for your aid,
Your strength and shield in me displayed.
So it is, and so shall be,
Your protection cloaking me.

Finally, return to awareness.
Slowly bring your focus back to your physical surroundings.

A Manual to Magical Resilience

To Call upon the Family of the Sun

Terrance Gamble

SHOULD A CHALLENGE PRESENT ITSELF that conventional ways can not conquer, nor divination clarify, nor even witchery provide an obvious solution for, then bring offerings to an altar to call upon the family of Lord Helios.

The Sun god of the Hellenic world was believed to have seen all things that occurred during the daytime, and so was a witness of truth. He fathered some of the Hellenic world's most famous witches including Kirke and was grandfather to Medea. Their blessings may be called upon to see one's way through great struggles. Give them an offering at night before bed that their answers may be given through dreams.

Either at an indoor altar or outside beneath the Moon, lay out a vessel of red wine or pomegranate juice, with a vessel of olive oil, and another of salt and another still, full of water. If you feel moved to burn candles for them and offer flowers, then do so. Light a candle to bring the presence of the goddess Hestia. Light three bay leaves with that flame and submerge them into a vessel of water and then wash your hands with that water. You may set this water aside beyond the sacred space with another offering of wine or juice which will appease profane spirits that dwell near.

When you feel ready, you may begin the recitation:

Let the witch family of Lord Helios turn their attention here.
May they find these offerings that I lay here favorable and pleasing.
Before Mother Earth below and Mother Night above,
To bare witness to this rite, let them come!

Lady Kirke, revealer of hidden truths.
She who brings forth the inner nature,

Serpents of Circe

Be welcome here Golden Eyed One,
As thy father shines his light as the crown jewel of upon the diadem of Hemera,
Bearing witness to all that transpires upon the Earth.
You may lead those you favor to the truth unseen, great Pharmakeia of Helios.
Let truth be mine, in exchange for these offerings.

Lady Pasiphae, exacter of justice.
She who is brings oathbreakers to their knees,
Be welcome here Mother of the Bull,
As thy husband broke the marriage vows spoke before Great Hera,
Your friends the banes and venoms brought him to heel.
You restore that which has been blighted by hubris, great Queen of Crete.
Let justice be mine, in exchange for these offerings.

Lord Aeetes, the master of cunning arts.
He who sets challenges that wisdom may be gained,
Be welcome here Lord of the Fleece,
As thy daughter worked her sharp wit against thy trials set for Jason,
You may lead those you favor to revelation should they meet the challenge.
Let cunning be mine, in exchange for these offerings.

Lady Medea, the beholder of arcane wisdom.
She who obtains her desires through the knowledge of the craft,
Be welcome here High Priestess of Hekate,
As thy father set trials before your lover and you used knowledge to undo them,
You who have great knowledge, please teach me oh benefactress of the strix.

A Manual to Magical Resilience

Let wisdom and knowledge by mine, in exchange for these offerings.

Lady Ariadne, the guide toward epiphany.
She who is ecstatic, struck with inspiration,
Be welcome here Mistress of the Maenads,
As thy spouse reveals the mysteries hidden within the self, the labyrinth,
You guide the seeker toward the center, to that which must be
   confronted.
Let revelation be mine, in exchange for these offerings.

Great witches born of Lord Helios, lay hands upon my brow and
send me aloft toward the realm of dreams. That misty world governed by
   Lord Hypnos
where your divine guidance may be met.

Pour out the offerings at a local crossroads and prepare yourself for bed.

A Spray a Day Keeps the Magic Your Way
Richard Levy

*P*HARMAKEIA, THE POWER OF THE HERBS AND ROOTS of the Earth fuelled by the great mother and having power over all she has birthed, this is what makes witches powerful and dangerous and awesome... and why the more skilled we are, the more we can do. Diffuser sprays are often used to clear auric energy and "atmospheres." That's all well and good, but they are much more multi-purposed than that and can be used to assist spell work of many kinds. From there you can add herbs and oils and bottle magic. You can easily create your own mixtures. Here are some to enjoy. In terms of amounts: less is more, follow your nose and let the herbs guide you—i.e., be a witch!

To make diffuser sprays, you will need a base to add herbs and oils to. Fill a bowl with water and add some vodka (just enough so it can last long but also to feed the spirits you work with). When making your mixture consider layering your spellwork with candles and incense and speak to the herbs the oils so they know the work you are doing with them. When everything is mixed, place your hands over the mixture and speak your intent, craft a prayer and incantation, and you can end with a chant, such as:

Thus this mixture now combine
Both earthly power and divine

If you work with crystals, you can place them in the mixture and let it sit for a while. Feel the power with your hands and mix the power with your hands. Let your mind be focused, still your core, and let your hands weave magic. You will feel when this is done. Then pour the mixture in a diffuser bottle to use at your will, or even buy small ones to carry 'round with you in your pocket. As witches you can work with

A Manual to Magical Resilience

this technique and adapt your own as well.

Let the power speak to you.

Here are some simple mixtures I have made in the past. You can consider floral waters and various approaches to make these potions. Always check for allergies and take care in relation to toxicity and how you or others may react to them. In general, these are safe, but always be vigilant in your craft. Feel free to make these your own and create new magic.

⚜ POLYPHARMAKOS

(Assists in all spellcasting)

Herb(s) to infuse in the base: Rosemary and Jasmine

Oils: Bergamot, Orange, Ylang

⚜ PROTECTION AND CLEANSING

(Purifies a space and draws in protection)

Herbs: Hyssop, nettle, and bay (some salt)

Oils: lavender

⚜ GOD OF THE WOODS

(so that nature can dwell where you are overloaded by people or work and to invoke nature)

Herbs: You an add some wood chips or leaves as a base but do mot use too much and consider what you are using e.g. Yew is poisonous so care is needed but what is growing around you and calls to you

Oils – sandalwood (3 drops), cedarwood (9 drops), dragon's blood (3 drops) – three oils from trees

Serpents of Circe

❧ GODDESS ENCHANTMENT

(for women to claim power in an environment or calling Goddesses)

Herbs: Rosemary and Rose

Oils: vanilla and Jasmine

❧ PANACEA'S TOUCH

(healing potion for spells both absent and present healing and for yourself, this is for universal Healing—when doing this a prayer to the Goddess Panacea is advised)

Herbs: chamomile and bay

Oils: Yarrow, eucalyptus, rose

❧ NECROMANCER'S HAND

(To help the dead who have passed unjustly but this will also assist necromancy)
Herbs: parsley and wormwood

Oils: Mugwort and Jasmine

❧ CIRCE'S SERPENT VENOM

(This is to carry the spirit of this book and its intended purpose—empowering your sorcery, transmutation, necromancy—to consider justice, protection, empowerment, banish anything unwanted and too provide balance) Note: I have chosen not to add poisons for safety and accessibility, but Mandrake would a go to and I have used when making this, its name in Greek being Kireka, named after Circe herself. Venom and poison to witches are not something to fear, but care is needed, and in this case I have named this mixture in line with this book and also because poisons and venoms are full of deep and dark enchantment and magic, transformative and potent.

A Manual to Magical Resilience

⇨ HERBS:

1. Dandelion: A solar plant to draw on her paternal magic (of her father Helios) and potent wish granter and spirit caller (add some root and flower)

2. Rosemary: whilst often a solar plant—so it partners well with Dandelion—her name means dew o' the sea, drawing on the power of water, connecting to Circe's mother Perse. Rosemary is also a great ally in all forms of witchcraft, a great protector and strong in feminine power it being a liminal plant full of magic.

3. A clove of garlic: when Odysseus came to Circe, he carried Moly (which means root) and it is hypothesised this is Garlic, so use a leaf or clove to add apotropaic magic and banishing to your mixture.

⇨ OILS:

1. Rose: balance and magic, rose is full of deep enchantment beyond love spells alone it invites blessings and elevation through the deep and dark enchantment of the Earth.

2. Vanilla: This brings luck and sensuality and pleasure in all things, be it erotic, magical, and in life bask in the things you want and let them come to you.

3. Jasmine is full of intense enchantment and now is not the time to shy from that.

4. Lotus: This is full of enchantment and heightens your psychic ability to compliment your Sorcery.

In blending this listen to the oils or consider what scent you feel should dominate the others or compliment etc this is about listening to your magic and your own dialogue with Circe.

A Petition to Isis

Victoria Raschke

THE NAVIGIUM ISIDIS, the Vessel of Isis festival, was an ancient Roman celebration of the end of winter and a time to call upon the goddess to prod politicians and leaders into doing right by the people they governed or to stand aside if they were unwilling or unable to do so. This ritual is usually done in early March as part of the festival, but I think Isis will understand we have great need in this season.

In book eleven of *Metamorphoses*, or *The Golden Ass*, Apuleius gives us the most information we have about the celebration of the Vessel of Isis festival. Lucius, the book's main character, is turned into a donkey in a spell gone wrong. After many adventures, he awakens at the edge of the sea. He prays to whomever may be listening that he be returned to his human form. In answer, Isis rises from the waves with a golden compass on her forehead. She instructs him to find the priest in the festival procession happening that day and to eat the roses the priest will be carrying. Lucius does as the goddess says and is turned back into a man. He then joins the procession of people dressed in white to the sea where a small boat has been prepared, marked with hieroglyphs and filled with gifts for the goddess Isis.

> YOU WILL NEED:
>
> a small brass compass (found at camping and outdoor stores)
>
> some bay leaves
>
> a wax crayon, soft graphite pencil, or non-toxic marker
>
> roses, preferably orange or white—for enthusiasm or purity—and not sprayed with pesticide

A Manual to Magical Resilience

your nearest body of water, or a basin or bowl of water if you need to do this at home

white clothing, or at least a white scarf or bandana to cover your head

On the morning of the 5th of March, or when the need arises, bathe and dress in white. Prepare the above items and proceed to your nearest body of water in whatever way that you can. If that is a bowl of water at your altar, so be it. Witches make do and do our best to include everyone.

When you reach your destination, sit or stand at the water's edge and ask Isis to help you sort out your most pressing issue. Use your crayon and bay leaves to write out a petition for yourself and petitions for the political leaders to do right by the people and the planet or get out of the way, allowing those who will to step up. Hold the bay leaves in your palm with the compass and recite your petitions aloud to Isis or whomever you may think is listening. Speak from your heart. Eat one of the rose petals—this is why it's important they are not sprayed—then walk into the water if possible or wash your hands or splash your face with the water. Float the bay leaves and the roses, your offering, on the surface.

As a representation of the divine guidance, you have requested for yourself and others, wash the compass in the water and take it with you. As you leave to return home, do not look back at your petitions and offering. If you've used a bowl or basin, leave your offering outside and pour the water onto the ground or dispose of the items thoughtfully in the trash or compost and give a houseplant a drink or pour the water down the kitchen drain. You can place the compass on your altar as a reminder or carry it with you when you work to hold those in power accountable, whatever that is for you. It can be organizing, protesting, voting, letter writing, donating funds, etc. Managing our part of this rite will look different for everyone.

Shifting Perspective Sigil

Laura Tempest Zakroff

BUILT INTO THIS SIGIL:

- ¶ a shift to more positive thinking
- ¶ greater acceptance and empathy towards others
- ¶ a willingness to expand understanding and connection
- ¶ kindness
- ¶ the ability to break away from negative or unhealthy spirals of thinking
- ¶ greater awareness of energy (of both self and others)

WHAT TO DO WITH THIS SIGIL: This is a very social sigil—it works best wherever people gather or exchange ideas (in person or online) to help make room for thoughtful change—especially wherever communication is taking place. Use with incense or place on a room spray infusion. You can place it as a screensaver on your devices or work into shared images. If you need to enact a shift within yourself, then apply it to your body using make-up, a body-safe marker, or anoint with an anointing oil that works in alignment with the sigil.

A Manual to Magical Resilience

Dear Transphobe, Thanks for the $400

Ron Padrón

I OFTEN LISTEN TO MELODIC METAL ON MY COMMUTE HOME, especially when I'm stressed. So there I am, rounding the corner after singing along with In Flames at the top of my lungs, letting the miles between my job and home work in tandem with the guitar riffs and drums to lift my spirits, when I see it: some anti-trans bullshit banner on a neighbor's car.

My mood sours immediately. I stop singing. I'm thankful the neighbor isn't outside so I don't have to perform the social ritual of performatively waving hello as I drive by. I honestly don't know if I could have restrained myself from giving them the finger. But then a random piece of trivia I haven't thought about in years pops up: Wunsiedel.

Wunsiedel is a small town in Germany and was once the resting place of top Nazi official, Rudolf Hess. His grave became a pilgrimage site for neo-Nazis, who would show up annually to commemorate his death. After years of putting up with this, the townsfolk came up with the great idea to turn the march into a fundraiser against extremism through an organization called Rechts gegen Rechts (Right against Right). For every meter the Nazis marched the townsfolk and local businesses would donate 10 Euros to EXIT Deutschland, an organization which helps people leave extremist groups.

I immediately hatch a plan, and as soon as I'm home I open my laptop and log into Facebook. A few minutes later I set up a fundraiser for TransLifeline, shared with a post describing the neighbors banner and how I'd like to thank them for helping to raise money to support trans folks. By the end of the fundraiser my community raised $400.

Circe is best known for her power of transformation. We have several stories of how, when met with unexpected obstacles, she uses her magic of transmutation to punish or outwit those who have crossed her—whether turning the unwelcome sailors who have defiled her sacred island into swine, turning a king who denied her affections into a woodpecker, or poisoning the bath of the naiad Scylla thus removing a love rival and transforming her into a terrifying sea monster. What a Circean approach to magic teaches us is the ability to take the things that would deny us, harm us, impede us and shift that energy into a new form.

In the story I shared above I took something that is all too common for those of us in the queer community—hate, intolerance, bigotry—and transformed it into something new—support, resources, and community. This is a practice that all communities pushed to the margins should learn to cultivate. How do we take the scorn and resentment of those who would seek to turn established systems against us, and instead redirect that energy into something we can use to access the resources, power, and connections we need in order to not only survive, but thrive.

A Manual to Magical Resilience

Lessons from Queen Nanny
SOLIDARITY & MUTUAL AID

Emma Kathryn

WHAT DOES IT MEAN TO BE AN OBEAH WOMAN, A WITCH? Rebellion and resistance flows through our very veins, as though the struggles of our kin have forged us in flame, strengthened us with an iron core. Our blood blazes white hot with victories hard won, readying us for the battles still to be fought. This is the essence of those who wield magic, a recognition of the power within, writhing with a growing hunger, in this, the age of the anthropocene.

Quite often such people stand alone, just on the outskirts of the "normal," the polite, the mundane. All the stories and lore of such folks point to lonely figures, misaligned by their communities, outcast and othered. And yet there is more, for has not the witch, the obeah practitioner, the magic wielder also been the last recourse, the last bastion of help? Have they not supported their communities when all other options have been tried and found lacking? Has not the witch always stood firm?

When I think about issues such as these, when I look out into the world, as beautiful and varied as it is, and see the hurt and seemingly hopelessness of endless wars, poverty and all, I can't help but think of one of my own heroes, Queen Nanny of the Maroons. Queen Nanny wasn't royalty, though some of the stories that have sprung up around the myth of the woman would suggest she was, she has become a national hero of Jamaica. Nanny was an enslaved woman, taken from her homeland of Ghana to Jamaica where she worked sugar plantations with other enslaved people. She was also an obeah woman, and it is this power that aided her to freedom.

When I'm being lazy, I describe obeah as Jamaican witchcraft, but the truth is obeah is a spiritual and magical system that has its roots in

Serpents of Circe

West Africa, but it transformed and became something else as it was transported with the enslaved into the Caribbean. Here, in this place where peoples from different tribes and countries were forced together in the bonds of slavery, ideas and beliefs mingled, and then mixed some more with Taino (the indigenous people of the Caribbean) ideas, beliefs and practices, and so obeah was reborn as an Afro-Caribbean magical system. Much like witchcraft, there are subtle differences in obeah wherever it is found in the islands, but the power and energy remain at the core.

Nanny was responsible for several revolts and uprisings within the plantation, but her story and mythos really came into their own when she finally managed to escape it. However, Nanny was not satisfied with her own freedom and so she worked to win the freedom of other enslaved peoples. She became a mighty military leader, proficient in guerilla warfare, and her power became well known and respected. She could stop the enemies bullets and heal her fighters with the power of obeah! Indeed her victories against the better equipped and more advanced British military was proof of her power to those who followed her.

Eventually, the British gave up their fight with Nanny, whose own community increased with each plantation attacked, awarding Nanny and her community of Maroons the freedom they had already taken for themselves. There is still a Maroon community in the mountains of Jamaica today, though obeah is still outlawed there and in other countries.

For me, Nanny's story mirrors the needs we still have today, in our own communities. While the specific circumstances have changed, there is still injustice that must be fought, and we witches, obeah practitioners and magicians are still at the forefront of the fight. We always have been. From Nanny's story, we can see the importance of solidarity with others, even when their struggles are not our own and that mutual aid is an important factor in fighting against injustice. Sometimes though, the hard part is figuring out how to get started, but fear not as forming our own solidarity and mutual aid networks can be easily done and in many ways for those willing to commit a little time and effort. Here I will share with you a few tips on how to get started!

Firstly, as the magical beings we are, consider where your craft can help. While there are so many spells and workings that can be called on and utilised, there are other ways in which your own flavour of magic can be useful. Can you help teach people and make simple remedies and medicines with your herbal know-how? I often hold foraging walks in my local town, which not only serves to teach people about the land where they live and identify useful and edible plants but also begins to build a small community of like minded people, a community that may be small but is growing. Or maybe you can help people manage their own frustrations and bring inner peace and calm with meditation practices? Can you use your magic to help people realise their own personal power, giving them strength and inspiration?

It's not only magic that can help us though it certainly has a role in empowering ourselves and others. Mutual aid can look like a lot of different things. It can look like forming small circles of people who can help in times of need. A friend of mine runs a dog shelter, and she has a small group of people who can respond to emergencies, and this idea of having a pool of people who can dip in and out as needed is one that can be useful as it requires only a little time and effort. But even before you get to forming groups, mutual aid can be so simple. You can hold potluck suppers for your neighbours, where everyone brings a little something to create a wonderful meal and also build the bonds of community and friendship. Or maybe you can hold a swap and share "sale," not only helping people but the planet as well.

The idea of community extends beyond our human selves and includes the land where we live and the other beings in that land. When I think of Nanny of the Maroons, I think about how the jungles and hills of Jamaica aided her in her fight against the British, how she was able to feed herself and her fighters, and heal them with the power of plants. As

Serpents of Circe

such, our solidarity and mutual aid is to the land as well, and helping to look after it helps the people too, for we are a part of it. Organising local litter picking events not only benefits the land but also works to bring people together. If you have specific local knowledge of the land and the animals that live there, maybe consider holding a class to help others see their local space as something alive with soul, spirit and magic.

As Queen Nanny reminds us, our magic should empower us to make the changes we want to see manifest in the world, and though the figure of the witch, obeah practitioner and magician are often outliers, we are also the ones capable of bringing people together to fight the good fight and win!

A Manual to Magical Resilience

Being Radically Resilient
A JOURNEY OF IDENTITY AND LIBERATION
Sawyer Massie & Adam Black

THE HISTORIES OF QUEER PEOPLE ARE A LIVING RECORD. We wear it on our flesh, hold it in our hearts and minds, and express it in the manners of our love. In these spaces of self-expression, we share ourselves and our histories with the world. It, in turn, responds. Here we meet our radical spirit. By moving in ways that challenge cultural norms and societal standards, we claim our spaces in culture and society. The overculture will inevitably respond. And react. But in these declarations of autonomy, there is another response. Through this visibility, queer individuals and groups may find themselves reflected in the world. There is a sense of belonging. This encourages perspectives to evolve from "I" to "we."

Our queer identities are often forged through self-motivated exploration, merging at the intersection of our drives and the influence of those who came before and walk alongside us as our chosen mentors, guides, and family. These chosen figures form a sense of belonging, providing models for living that address our needs juxtaposed with the heterocentric models many queer people are raised in. And it is here we meet our resilient spirit. Through our hardships, we are empowered to find, identify, and know ourselves. We find and build community. We bring together and share culture. Those skills of adaptability we honed to survive and maintain become the fire and passion that evolve into our ability for transformation.

We are alchemists, but our transformation is never a solitary endeavor. The work is our own, to which we are personally accountable, but we are carrying our healing and new ways of being into the world. This visibility again affects change in our communities and expands

Serpents of Circe

outward into society. We move our histories forward. And inevitably through our culture and shared histories, we solidify our lineages and a shared lineage. We bring forward models for future generations that are better equipped to provide a foundation in which to explore, own and love their queerness, celebrate their milestones, and share this onward to future generations to do the same.

The absolute beauty of our queer community and communities is its expansive, inclusive nature. With respect to our communities and individual identities, that "+" in LGBTQIAP+ is paramount. The creation and evolution of this acronym implies, regardless of its initial state, we were all outsiders at one point but there is infinite space for others. Life and love are perpetually in motion. In seeing ourselves outwardly reflected, we move in ways that are more kind, loving, and forgiving of ourselves. And if we can gift this to ourselves, we can share this gift with others. And we can continue to affirm ourselves and one another through this radical resilience.

Radical resilience, as it is understood in this context, is an intentional bridging of self as an integral component to our communities, nature, and existence as a whole. All are necessary components. It is a quality of being whole in oneself, recognizing this in others, and holding space and supporting them in their journeys. It is an act of healing that encourages us to move beyond survival to thrive. For ourselves and one another.

From this perspective, our identities, expression, and lives become purposeful challenges to the overculture and its oppressive systems for the sake of our queer siblings. The purpose is no longer just a matter of visibility, which will always be necessary, but something of action. This sense of radical resilience can inspire us to find our voices and move into leadership roles on behalf of our communities to encourage autonomy, advocate for social change and equitable treatment, and empower queer people to live in accordance with our natures, values, and realities.

A Manual to Magical Resilience

And as we lean further into this expression, having absorbed, integrated, and evolved with our queer upbringing, we build on the foundations of our elders and mentors to live authentic, unapologetically queer lives that emphasize our place as the central figures in control of our narratives. This presents us the opportunity to know nature and its processes through the lens of our experiences. This brings together language, symbolism, customs, and rituals that are applicable and understandable within the context of our lives. We consolidate these into perspectives and worldviews that support our well-being.

We are dynamic. Our history is rich, our present is an unfolding journey, and the future is ours to shape. We are, or we can be, the heroes in our own stories. When we prioritize ourselves, we make definitive stances for our well-being and betterment. Not at the expense of others, but because our position is no less important. When we empower ourselves, we empower one another. We take our circumstances and from them we make gold. And when we come together in solidarity, whole in ourselves, we stand firmly rooted in our autonomy and ready to face the world. Together.

Serpents of Circe

We Are Nothing Without our Dead

Ron Padrón

WHAT MAKES A COMMUNITY? It is more than physicality and geographic proximity, although that often helps. A community is made by those who share a common cause. By those who freely share what they have with each other, be it knowledge, resources, labor, or a safe space. A community often shares a common history or, at least, one in which its members have enough overlap as to feel part of the same story.

A community is also made of the dead.

They are those who have come before. Those who have made possible what we have now, sometimes at the cost of their own life. They are the individual threads that reach back into a shared past, weaving a history that tells us who and what we are.

We cannot truly be a community unless we are *in community* with our dead. This is why systems such as colonialism, fascism, and nationalism try so hard to control history in order to sever communities deemed malignant from their dead. Absent our ancestors we exist in a vacuum, with no past and therefore no future. This is why African families were broken and scattered in the slave trade. This is why far-right politicians try to keep everything queer locked in a closet by criminalizing LGBTQ+ history and identity.

In *The Odyssey*, Circe tells Odysseus that he must travel to the Underworld to seek the counsel of the dead in order to determine how to appease the gods so he can finally return home. In this example, the dead serve as intermediaries between humans and the divine. The knowledge and experience they have from being on the other side of the veil grants them wisdom the living cannot yet access. While Odysseus had to seek out the entrance to the Underworld, we can bring that entrance to us. Below you will find some tips on establishing an Ancestor

A Manual to Magical Resilience

Shrine that can serve as an anchor for the dead in your community. This shrine serves as both a physical, visual reminder of their existence and memory and a powerful magical focus for ritual work that seeks the wisdom, protection, and blessings of our ancestors.

HOW TO BUILD

First, you need to build your community ancestor shrine. Here are some things to think about.

¶ What do you envision when you think of an ancestor shrine? Maybe you envision a sacred tree in a clearing. Or maybe you think of a small structure, like a bird house, nestled among the flowers in your backyard. ¶ When creating your community ancestor shrine, think deeply about its various components. Do you want to use something natural, like wood or stone? Is it important for it to be something living? You might consider marking a specific tree or garden as your shrine. Or, maybe you want to designate a room or specific structure as the shrine. You can fill it with photos, clothing, or anything else that represents those who have passed. ¶ How is the shrine decorated? Are there specific colors you want to use or avoid? Do you want to incorporate the use of runes or sigils to anchor the intent and purpose of the shrine? Does your shrine need a place for offerings, live plants, candles, etc.?

HOW TO WARD

Second, it's time to protect your shrine. Whatever you've created is serving as a literal anchor to the other side. It's a beacon to the dead, so make sure the right ones see it. Also, make sure the dead don't wander off.

¶ Your shrine is acting as a type of spirit house or spirit telephone. You want to make sure only the type of spirits you want have access to this shrine and the people who will use it. It's a good idea to engage the community in deciding what these wards will be—sigils, runes, some-

thing buried in the ground, a ritually maintained circle, etc.—and in the initial creation. The creation of the wards should be tied into whatever ritual or celebration you use to initially sanctify, or "open", this shrine.
¶ Maintain your shrine, both physically and energetically. Cleaning the shrine is just good manners, but it can also be an offering of service to your ancestors. Remove litter, dead plants, and anything else that shouldn't be there. Also make sure you routinely energetically cleanse the shrine. This will ensure ambient energy doesn't build up and make being in communion with your ancestors more difficult, but it can also clear out any negative energy left behind by those visiting the shrine.
¶ If the shrine is somewhere public or easily accessible it might be a good idea to add in additional warding to protect it from vandalism or desecration. Depending on where the shrine is situated, this could also be tied into a more traditional security system such as an alarm panel or security cameras. ¶ Clearly mark the boundaries of the sacred space created by the shrine that allows easier access to speaking with your ancestors. If the shrine is a room or a building that answer might seem pretty clear. However, if it's a tree, rock, or art installation, you will have to seriously consider the three-dimensional space you are creating. This helps demarcate mundane and sacred space for use of the shrine for personal reflections or group rituals. You are setting a "fence" for the spirits attracted by the shrine. The last thing you want, I'm assuming, is for this anchor to serve as an open door letting anything come through and go wandering about. ¶ If you are concerned about creating something that is passively "open for business" you might consider establishing a formal process for opening and closing the shrine. If you go this route, is this process something everyone knows and can do? Or is there someone, or a group of people, who will serve as dedicated shrinetenders who help facilitate connection with the ancestors, and who are responsible for managing the bridge between worlds?

A Manual to Magical Resilience

Ancestral Spiderweb Ward
A SPELL FOR RESILIENCE
Elhoim Leafar

HARD TIMES CAN OFTEN BRING OUT THE WORST in people who negatively bombard us. Like spiders, we can transform this negativity. Spiders feed on the insects they trap in their webs and, through a fascinating biological (and perhaps alchemical) process, expel spider silk—a protein fiber used to create their webs. These webs capture prey and allow spiders to swing and maneuver.

As nature's alchemists, spiders convert the bodies of smaller insects like flies and worms into more spider silk, attracting even more prey. They create something beautiful and powerful from negativity.

In the Amazon, snake skin, readily available near the river each morning, would be used for this purpose. However, large cities also possess a powerful magic we often underestimate. Here, I've utilized spiderwebs for my spell. This is especially effective for spells that use negative emotions as fuel, like the one I created during the Me Too and Black Lives Matter protests—a spell designed to protect protestors.

THE SPELL

This simple and easy-to-do spell draws upon the strength and resilience of ancestors, the protective nature of spiders, and the focused power of the sorcerer's jar to create a ward against negativity and harmful magic.

INGREDIENTS:

❧ Sorcerer's Jar: A clear jar or container for this purpose.

❧ Incense: You can use an ethically resourced incense stick or cone of your preference or just create your loose mix using some kitchen

Serpents of Circe

dry herbs and burn them carefully over charcoal.

⇨ Spiderwebs: Gathered ethically, without harming the spider. You can use the delicate outer webs or collect molted casings.

⇨ Yarn or string: If you can't find any spiderwebs or a 10-20cm cutting long from a natural vine.

⇨ Black Obsidian: A small, polished piece for deflecting negativity.~ A black candle and (optional) a white candle.

⇨ Soil from the local land: If you feel connected to a place where your ancestors lived, a pinch of soil can be a powerful addition. If not, simply grab a bit of soil from any local park.

⇨ Herbs for Protection (Choose one or combine a few):

* Rosemary (cleansing, protection)
* Rue (warding off evil)
* Basil (courage, strength)
* Mugwort (psychic protection)

⇨ Black Salt (Kala Namak) or Sea Salt: For purification and grounding.

RITUAL PREPARATION

After sunset, shower and prepare as you usually do for your ritual. Dress comfortably, and take slow, deep breaths a couple of times before you begin. Light the incense and, if you wish (optional), put a white candle on your altar.

INSTRUCTIONS

Cleanse the jar and all the ingredients with smoke from your incense. Hold each item in your hands, visualizing white light infusing them with your protective energy.

A Manual to Magical Resilience

Place the black obsidian at the bottom of the jar. Sprinkle a thin layer of the soil on top. Add the spiderwebs and chosen herbs.

Light a black candle and hold your hands over the jar. Visualize a swirling vortex of protective energy fueled by your ancestors' strength and the spider's resilience. See this energy infusing the jar and overflowing to create a shield around yourself and the people you're casting for.

Chant or recite an affirmation, putting your power and intent into the words. Here's an example of the one I use, which you can repeat or modify to make your own.

> *From the land's spirit, I draw strength anew,*
> *Circe's cunning whispers guide me through.*
> *By the webs of resilience, my ancestors spun,*
> *A shield I weave following the setting sun.*
> *Spidercob, a gift of tiny might,*
> *Entangles foes in the shadows of the night.*
> *Protected and unstoppable, my spirit takes a stand,*
> *Love's fierce flame burns any evil hand.*

Drizzle the salts over the contents and firmly seal the jar. You can use wax, cloth, or any other appropriate method. Keep the jar sealed and safe in a dark place where nobody else can see it. If this spell is made to cast a protective spell in a specific location, be sure to be able to hide it in that location.

Using an App to Grow Closer during Times of Adversity
Enfys J. Book

AS WE CULTIVATE COMMUNITIES OF MAGICKAL RESILIENCE, we must intentionally build communication structures that can help us deepen our community connections in the face of adversity. Here's a story of how my coven did exactly that.During the COVID-19 lockdown in 2020–2021, my coven, like many other magickal groups, opted to stop meeting in person until we all had the chance to get fully vaccinated. As the coven high priestx, I was concerned that our group of seven 40- to 65-year-olds, including three brand-new members, would grow emotionally distant when we stopped spending time together in the same physical space. But, amazingly, the opposite happened: we grew closer than we'd been before lockdown.

I had been using a free video voicemail app to connect with faraway friends well before the pandemic. It was perfect when I was traveling abroad to send quick messages to my partner, because our timezones didn't match up well for synchronous conversations.

I noticed the app had a group chat feature and thought it was worth a try with the coven, as a way to keep us connected during lockdown. Not everyone in the coven is terribly techno-savvy, but thankfully they were all willing to give it a try.

We laid down a few ground rules early on:

1. Nobody is under obligation to participate.

2. Nobody is under obligation to view every single message, or to keep up with the app daily or even weekly. Therefore, if something time-sensitive needs to be addressed, use text messaging to reach leadership. And if something important but not time-sensitive needs the ears of the whole group, use our group email list.

A Manual to Magical Resilience

To my pleasant surprise, everyone decided to participate, and people dove in with relish. We were all starved for socialization in the depths of the pandemic, so seeing and hearing each other, instead of just reading each other's words on a screen, and having a platform for casual, social conversation people could participate in whenever they had time to do so, proved to be a welcome addition to every convener's life. It made me so happy to see my covenmates sharing bits of their lives with each other and having spiritual conversations, showing things they'd made, letting their kids say hi, and just generally relating to each other in the middle of their daily lives in a way they hadn't done previously.

And as I write this, in 2024, our coven still uses the app as a supplementary means of casual conversation, even though we're back to meeting for ritual in person. The quick-and-easy nature of just saying a thing vs. typing it, of getting to see people's facial expressions and the nuance of their tone of voice, and getting to show off things we're proud of, makes this app really work for us.

Video voicemail is not only friendly to folks with super busy schedules, but also for many folks with chronic health issues, mental illnesses, and different neurotypes. The async nature of the app makes it easier for people with limited energy and social bandwidth to participate when they have the spoons to do so, in short bursts rather than committing to an extended get-together or long phone or video chat. Those who struggle with eye contact or with showing their face on video can drop a simple text message in the app, or a photo, or a photo with a voiceover, if they prefer. There are lots of ways to participate.

The video voicemail app my coven uses is called Marco Polo. It may not be around forever, of course (which is why I didn't name it at the beginning of the article), and may not be your preferred app of choice, but I think there's a lot of advantage to connecting a small spiritual group with async video. I encourage you to think through how your spiritual groups can stay connected when you can't physically be together. For example, larger groups may want to consider setting up smaller groups within the group to connect in this manner, so the number of messages doesn't get overwhelming. Or you may find other online tools work better for your group's particular techno-savvy and comfort levels. The important thing is that we find more ways to include people in an async fashion, which can help us broaden our community reach to include people with mobility and logistical limitations to attending events in person. Our connections to our community can and should become deeper than what we can achieve when we limit our interactions to in-person events. Video voicemail and other online tools can give us a more holistic approach to connecting members of our community.

A Manual to Magical Resilience

Where Do I Go from Here?

Dave Gaddy,
The Weathered Wiseman

Where do I go from here, I ask the night,
Under the moon's soft, questioning light.
The paths before me, tangled and vast,
Stretch into shadows, recalling the past.
The whispers of dreams, of futures unknown,
Echo through silence, where seeds have been sown.
Stars above shimmer, guiding yet still,
Heartbeats of hope, to answer fate's will.
Do I wander the meadows, seek the dawn's glow,
Or delve into forests, where mysteries grow?
Shall I scale mountains, chase the high skies,
Or linger by rivers, where truth quietly lies?
Each step is a choice, each breath a plea,
For the courage to venture, for my eyes to see.
In the journey of life, where paths interlace,
Each step leads somewhere, adventures in place.
So, where do I go from here, I sigh,
With wings to unfurl, with dreams to try.
The journey awaits, with its laughter and tears,
Forward, onward, despite all fears.

The Aequitas Sigil

Laura Tempest Zakroff

BUILT INTO THIS SIGIL:

- circuit of truth prevailing and energizing change
- restructure/regain healthy balance within the framework and maintaining it
- summoning of consequences for those working against the whole of the people, and the removal of the compromised
- change from the root level to the top in line with the needs of the future
- invoking the aid and essence of Justice in all Her forms and the Mighty Dead
- protection of the people
- installing of judges who are of the people
- fairness, fruitfulness, equity and equality engaged and thriving
- trident to rule fairly, torch to illuminate the way
- reduce the influence of fascism, fundamentalism, and the 1%

WHAT TO DO WITH THIS SIGIL: Apply the sigil with black ink to a white candle and call upon a Justice-related deity, ancestor, or spirit.

The Work of Us, In This Moment

Alicia "Jynx" Vervain

I take a breath into this moment
into this place
to remind myself
of some important truths:

That water collects on the grass in the mornings,
and that air feeds embers into roaring flames
stark against the blue-black of night.

That flowers bloom in the Spring
and leaves die in the Fall;
That Winter always feels longest
when we're halfway through,
and that Summer never feels
long enough.

That a young one's laughter
is one of the most beautiful sounds
in all of existence
and that in order for family to mean anything,
it must be what we make of it.

I must remember
that there is iron in the earth
and iron in the stars
and iron in my blood, all the same.
I remember that I am connected with all things
and that this gives me both

Serpents of Circe

a sacred gift and a weighty responsibility
of stewardship and right relationship
with the land and the spirits
that intertwine with it
and will continue to do so
long after I am gone.

I must remember that our earth cannot be shaken
from the pain humans have wrought
upon it and each other
but that we can acknowledge
and make reparations to this land
and our history
and the past and lived history
of those who came before,
and those who are still here to this day.
And that in order to live in service to
the Greatest Good,
we must.

This is the magic of The Now:
to see the world as it is,
to listen beyond the shadow of my ego
or my society's ego
to what it needs,
and to learn how I may be a better human being
so that whatever parts and paths of this world
I may cross may be left better
and more balanced for those who come after.

I must remember that, as a human being,
I am not separate from this world,

A Manual to Magical Resilience

but of this world
and just as subject to the laws
of love and lifeand death and decay.

This is as it should be.

Some of these truths are
uncomfortable;
others inspiring.
All are necessary.

So as I breathe into this moment
into this place,
I ask that every time I sit here
and do this work
and say these words
that it get easier, more natural for me
to be here,
and live this work,
and feel these truths
in the deepest core
of my being.

And may I learn to be comfortable
with the discomfort
and inspired by the feeling of growth.

Because the change
starts
here.

And so it is.

Serpents of Circe

Acknowledgments

LAURA TEMPEST ZAKROFF:

EARLIER THIS YEAR I POSTED A THREAD ONLINE about ideas on how to maintain one's sanity and focus when there's so much we feel called to help with. Ron said to me something along the lines of "that sounds like another installment in the *New Aradia* series." I think replied with "Well, I'll let you know when that happens and you can be a part of it." It could be that this book is all Ron's fault, or it was the muses (spirits, deities, ancestors, etc) poking it deeper, or perhaps they had it out for both of us, but basically I woke up one day with that familiar inkling of an urge and the clear call of "it is time." I reached out to the ever-amazing Jenn Zahrt to share the message. In her unflappable and direct way, she quickly replied with, "So what's our focus and timeline?" I relayed the concept of shifting from resistance to resilience because I sensed that's what we will need the most in the days to come.

From the time of the seed idea through submissions and layout, I am in awe of not only what folks have brought to the table for this volume, but what we're experiencing on a larger scale culturally across the world. The Serpent is reaching for the Star. Change is afoot and we're ready for it. Thank you to everyone who has participated in the process along the way and to all those who will be inspired by what we've collected here. Together, we make magic that heals the past, awakens the present, and inspires the future.

REV. RON PADRÓN:

I'VE BEEN TOLD THAT THIS BOOK MIGHT BE MY FAULT. And I'm okay with that. I've been an activist in queer and disabled spaces for a while now, and a few years ago I finally hit that point of burn out that is so far past *actual burn out* that your body just stops. My approach and understanding of activism, advocacy, and radical reimagining of the

A Manual to Magical Resilience

world was rooted in the ebb and flow of offense and defense. Since then I've come to learn more about the importance of rest, healing, and the part of community-building that emphasizes making sure folks have a place they can catch their breath. I'm incredibly honored to be part of a volume that focuses on the important work of resilience, making sure we create safe and secure spaces for our most vulnerable, and the weaving of magic to continue transforming the world into a better place.

I'm incredibly thankful to Laura for inviting me on this journey, and for letting me contribute in my own way to *The New Aradia* series. I offer my thanks as well to Jenn Zahrt, for her patience in answering all the questions I had in my first journey in publishing and for modeling a deeply thoughtful process in creating this book. Most of all, thank you to everyone who answered the call to submit something for this book. The response was overwhelming, and whether your work was selected or not, it was incredible to see all of the magic y'all are bringing into the world.

Serpents of Circe

Contributors

Adam Black is an Initiate of the Unnamed Path, is a fervent practitioner of folk magic and traditional witchcraft. His dedication to the spiritual journey runs deep as he explores the intricate tapestry of gay male mysteries. Adam is on a mission to guide and empower the LGBTQ+ community, aiding them in reconnecting with forgotten mythos and tapping into latent magic.

Alicia "Jynx" Vervain is a passionate writer, poet, storyteller, & ritual dramatist, crafting language as a spiritual offering and as a means of better coming to know Deity & Self. The foundation of her Craft is the importance of Story & Myth in understanding not only who we are and who we've been, but also who we have the potential to be. Her practice is rooted in devotional poetry, dreamwork, bibliomancy, rhapsodomancy, and sex magic. A passionate researcher, belly dancer, full-spectrum doula, and activist for comprehensive sex education and reproductive rights, Jynx works primarily with Persephone, Inanna, the Dead, and her Self.

Christopher Michael is a self-identified witch with a lifelong love for magic in its many forms. Creative writing was a childhood passion of theirs that was packed tightly away until quite recently. By trade, Christopher is a holistic healing practitioner that employs an array of tools including several energy healing modalities, tarot, astrology, sound healing, and herbalism. They use these instruments to assist others in healing themselves, taking into account body, mind, and spirit. Christopher hopes to inspire others to live as their authentic self and work towards collective liberation. You can connect with them on Instagram, @mrchristophermichael

Claire Christine Sargenti is a New Orleans artist, activist and witch. Her work has been seen at the Ogden Museum of Southern Art, New Orleans Museum of Art, as well as in galleries, theaters, print publications and digital spaces across North America and Europe. She is a certified crystal therapist and the creator of the *Noble Moon Tarot Deck & Grimoire*. Follow her on Instagram at @clairevoyantspirit or on the web at xoclaireart.com

A Manual to Magical Resilience

Meet *Dave Gaddy*, a Southern male wytch whose journey through the realms of magick and spirituality has captivated hearts. Hailing from North Carolina and currently living in Atlanta, Gaddy blends his ancestral roots with the ancient craft, infusing his practice with a unique Southern charm. With a deep connection to nature, he navigates the realms of folklore, spellwork, and a passion for ancestral magick, sharing his insights in a way that resonates with the soul. Gaddy has been a practicing wytch for over 30 years and prior to following his magickal path was an ordained minister in two mainline denominations. Gaddy uses this background to enhance and strengthen his magickal practices the way his ancestors did with folk magick.

Elhoim Leafar is an urban spiritual worker, traditional brujo, and sorcerer from Amazonas, Venezuela. A professional dowser and tarot reader raised among curanderos, spiritists, and fortune tellers near the Orinoco River. Elhoim is a multi-traditionalist witch initiated into Candomble, Santeria, and 'Espiritismo Venezolano,' where he served the cult of Queen Maria Lionza on the mountain of Sorte (Yaracuy) and was a channeler/member for the 'Court of Witches. He was initiated into the esoteric Amazonian court of 'Los Encantados' dedicated to channeling, healing, and studying nature pre-Christian spirits. He is part of the Minoan Brotherhood of Witchcraft in New York.

Elyse Welles is a Greek-Egyptian American earth intuitive witch, podcaster, and author based in Athens, Greece. A practicing witch for over twelve years on three continents, she is a Priestess of the eclectic Faery Tradition. She writes regularly for *Witchology*, *Witch Way Magazine*, and the *Wild Hunt*, co-hosts the Magick Kitchen Podcast, and runs Seeking Numina, giving tours to Greece's sacred sites and teaching magical living in nature through connection to land spirits and spirits of place. She is an intuitive tarot reader. Read her works and sign up for her newsletter at seekingnumina.com + follow her on Instagram @seekingnumina.

Emiliano Russo has an MA in Anthropology, a degree in English culture and translation, and is a theater director graduated from the National Academy of Dramatic Arts. Since 2020 he has dedicated himself to the activity of blogger and digital creator, founding *L'Almanacco delle Streghe*, a portal that quickly became a reference point for many Italian witches. He is an initiate of the

Serpents of Circe

Temple of Ara Tradition. Among his teachers there are Phyllis Curott; Sorita d'Este; Emily Carding, Laura Tempest Zakroff and others. He holds different courses of magickal and personal growth. He's the author of *La Voce di una Stega*; *L'Agenda della Mela: la Magia della Luna*, a magickal journal with a note by Phyllis Curott. He is a columnist for *Witches Magazine*, a British quarterly written by witches for witches; and in 2022 he contributed to *The Gorgon's Guide to Magical Resistance*.

Emma Kathryn is a witch and obeah woman living in Robin Hood county in the UK. She is also an author with works published by Gods & Radicals Press and Llewellyn Worldwide. Through her works, Emma seeks to empower others to find the magic in the mundane. Her latest book, *Season Songs* (Llewellyn) aims to connect us to nature and each other in an animist revolution!

Enfys J. Book (they/them) is the author of the *Queer Qabala*, co-author of *Sagittarius Witch*, and author of the forthcoming *Queer Rites: A Magickal Grimoire to Honor Your Milestones with Pride* (Llewellyn, 2025). They are the High Priestx of the Fellowship of the Ancient White Stag coven near Washington, DC. Enfys has taught classes on magickal practice around the world. They are also the creator of majorarqueerna.com, a website devoted to queer magickal practice, and host a podcast called "4 Quick Q's: Book Talk with Enfys," where they interview pagan authors using a D20.

Irisanya Moon (she/they) is an author of 9+ books, Witch, priestess, international teacher, and initiate in the Reclaiming tradition. A devotee of Aphrodite, Hecate, the Norns, and Iris, she has practiced magick for 20+ years. They are passionate about the idea that life is and we are love spells, ever experiencing a dance of desire and connection, moving in and out of the heart, always returning to love. Her teaching/facilitation style is immersive, gracious, safe, and welcoming. (And her book on Circe arrives in the Fall of 2024). www.irisanyamoon.com

Ivo Dominguez Jr. has been active in the Pagan community since 1978. Ivo is an Elder in the Assembly of the Sacred Wheel. Ivo is the author of *The Four Elements of the Wise*; *Keys to Perception: A Practical Guide to Psychic Development*; *Practical Astrology for Witches and Pagans*; *Casting Sacred Space*; and

A Manual to Magical Resilience

Spirit Speak. He is the anchor author for the new twelve book *Witch's Sun Sign Series*. In his mundane life, he has been a computer programmer, the executive director of an AIDS/HIV service organization, a bookstore owner, and more.

J. R. Mascaro is an author, artist, and sorcerer who has been working with energy and communicating with inhabitants of the subtle realm since childhood. He has used his ritual practice to navigate life, and it is his desire to share with others his techniques and methods. J.R. holds a BA in Anthropology with a concentration in Anthropology of Religion and is a member of the Covenant of Unitarian Universalist Pagans. He is the author of *Seal, Sigil & Call: A New Approach to Ritual Magic* from Llewellyn Books, and is available for private consultations.

Joey Morris is a pink-haired floof mama, a Celtic Hedge Witch, Priestess of the Morrigan, author, and creatrix behind Starryeyedsupplies. Having studied history and mythology at university, these are still beloved areas of interest that weave their way into her modern Celtic witchcraft practice which has become an online sacred grove practice shared with the world.

Julie Nowak (she/they) is a multiply-disabled and neuroqueer educator, consultant, and writer based near Tkaronto (Toronto, Canada). Through their project "The Seasonal Body," Julie explores the intersection of disability justice, nature connection, food justice, and body liberation. They help institutions and individuals learn how to make nature connection more accessible. Julie is a white person with Celtic and Germanic ancestry. They view both the #LandBack movement and ancestral connection as important for nature-related work. You can follow Julie at SeasonalBody.org and @TheSeasonalBody on social media.

Kajira Djoumahna is a queer Modern Traditional Witch who lives with their husband of 33+ years, an exceedingly elderly cat, and a couple of bonsai trees in Northern California. A retired dance instructor and festival producer, Kajira has been involved with the pagan community for most of their life. She enjoys intentionally creating crafts such as candles, tying knots and painting rocks, jigsaw puzzling and celebrating holidays solo or with friends and cohorts.

Serpents of Circe

Kerri A. Horine is an instructor at Bellarmine University and Jefferson Community and Technical College. She graduated from the University of Louisville with an MA in English Literature, with a focus on Anaïs Nin and Surrealism, and a PhD in Humanities, with a focus on art history and spectacle. Along with academic articles, her writing and art have been included in Laura Tempest Zakroff's books, *Visual Alchemy* (2022) and *The Gorgon's Guide to Magical Resistance* (2022). Her paintings have been exhibited in numerous local group and solo shows, and she enjoys meditation and Dharma study.

Laura Tempest Zakroff (she/they) is a professional artist, author, performer, and Modern Traditional Witch based in New England. Laura is the author of several bestselling Llewellyn books including *Weave the Liminal*, *Sigil Witchery*, *Visual Alchemy*, and *Anatomy of a Witch*, as well as the artist and author of the *Anatomy of a Witch Oracle* and *The Liminal Spirits Oracle*. Laura edited *The New Aradia: A Witch's Handbook to Magical Resistance* and the *Gorgon's Guide to Magical Resistance* from Revelore Press. LTZ is the main creative force behind #WeAreAradia movement, organizes multiple community events, and teaches workshops online and worldwide. www.lauratempestzakroff.com

Luxa Strata is an artist, magican, and host of Lux Occult podcast; the creator / lead organizer of The Green Mushroom hypho-sigil project: a large-scale, ongoing group magical operation and working group focused on connection, creativity, and empowering individuals through the use of magic and esoteric technology; and Void House, aimed at creating a consent-forward magical space and providing consent education to the magically inclined. Luxa has been a lifetime magical practitioner with a background in art and science. Luxa has led public rituals, classes, and workshops about many magical topics / techniques and helps to facilitate weekly Discord chats about magic.

Mat Auryn, a bestselling multi-award winning author known for his books *Psychic Witch*, *Mastering Magick*, and *The Psychic Art of Tarot*, has gained recognition as a dedicated occult writer and educator. In addition to his solo works, he co-authored Pisces Witch with Ivo Dominguez, Jr., and has contributed to a range of respected esoteric publications. Mat is the co-host of THE CIRCLE IS podCAST alongside actress Rachel True, where they

A Manual to Magical Resilience

explore modern witchcraft and psychic development. He also teaches at the Omega Institute, co-owns Datura Trading Co., and is a co-founder of Modern Witch University in California's Bay Area, making significant contributions to the global witchcraft community. His books have been translated in over 13 languages across the world.

Michelle Cunningham is a writer, queer witch, folk magic practitioner, and lover of stones. Michelle has been following a Pagan path for more than 25 years and holds particular affinity with the geological landscape. She has facilitated workshops on stone witchcraft in Canada and the UK, and can currently be found teaching classes on fossil folklore and mineral magic at www.oldstoneways.com and on Instagram @oldstoneways. Michelle resides with her wife and fluffy black cat on the liminal edge of vast wilderness on traditional, unceded Coast Salish territory.

Moss Matthey is an author with Llewellyn and Moon Books, a contributor to various zines, and a regular speaker at Pagan events. Having been raised in a Fundamentalist Christian cult, he is now a Witch, Druid and Guardian of the Doreen Valiente Foundation. When he's not busy writing or doing witchy things, he likes to make videos for social media with his fairy which you can find on Instagram and TikTok.

The Rev. Dr. *P. Sufenas Virius Lupus* (e/em/eir/eirs/emself) is a metagender person, a Deity-spouse of Thetis (and parent to the semi-divine Echidnos from that coupling!) and spirit-spouse to two other beings, a devotee of Antinous, and a polytheist practitioner for over thirty-two years. E was a founder of modern Antinoan devotion, as well as foster-parent of the Tetrad++ Deities, and practices a queer, syncretistic, reconstructionist methodological practice in maintaining a Shrine to a variety of Deities and divine beings. A *fili* (poet/scholar), e publishes poetry, essays, books, and short fiction regularly, including in *The Gorgon's Guide to Magical Resistance*. http://psufenasviriuslupus.wordpress.com

Phoenix LeFae (she/her) started her journey in the world of Witchcraft in 1993 when her athame was a wooden-handled butter knife stolen from her mom's kitchen. Her love of magick and mystery has led her down many

Serpents of Circe

paths, lineages, and traditions. She is an initiate in the Reclaiming Tradition of Witchcraft, the Avalon Druid Order, and Gardnerian Wicca. Phoenix has written several books including *What Is Remembered Lives, A Witch's Guide to Creating and Performing Rituals, Witches, Heretics, and Warrior Women* and more. She is a professional Witch and the owner of the esoteric Goddess shop, Milk & Honey, (www.Milk-and-Honey.com).

Raven Edgewalker is a queer British Witch, teacher, artist and writer who lives in Somerset, UK. Raven sees their work in the world as that of building relationship, with self, within community, the natural world, with deity and with all seen and unseen beings. Raven has spent many years learning from the land and its creatures and listening to their voices; Though their work they hope to guide others to open to deeper relationships of their own. Raven is a collector of unconsidered trifles, an Ogham geek, Peacock devotee, and a tree-loving polytheist. Find them at greenwomancrafts.etsy.com and worldtreelyceum.org

Richard Levy is a witch in the UK who has been practicing over decades with earliest memories being a draw to witches and all things magic – and essentially not growing up and pursing this interest. Richard has a degree in philosophy and the theology and has a deep love of narrative and stories and due to this love, he performs storytelling. He has a deep love of Witchcraft and practices various forms of magic and among them the powers of herbs and plants. You can find Richard on Instagram under Pharmakeia_Uk where he shared his craft and engages with the community.

Rev. *Ron Padrón* (he/him/his) is the creator of White Rose Witching. He is a gay Cuban-American hedge priest from the swamps of Florida, now living in the mid-Atlantic with his husband and their small werewolf. He is specifically interested in divination, Queer Ancestor veneration and necromancy, hedge witchery, and spiritual activism. He has presented at gatherings such as the Salem Witchcraft and Folklore Festival, Hallowed Homecoming, Free Spirit Gathering, and Sacred Space. He is also a founder and co-editor of a punk spirituality zine, ALTAR PUNK, which is an interfaith project focused on reclaiming faith and spirituality from nationalist movements.

A Manual to Magical Resilience

Sawyer Massie is an initiate and teacher of Unnamed Path, a spiritual tradition for Men Who Love Men. His foundation is gay / queer spirituality and ecstatic animism. A warlock and folk magician, he is also a practitioner of folk magic, folkloric witchcraft, and chaos magic. Sawyer is passionate about connecting, empowering, and supporting men who love men and other members of the LGBTQIAP+ community in their spiritual journeys.

Shannon Rose Raison (she/her) is a queer femme of white settler ancestry. Her people are from the lands now known as Poland, Ireland, England, and Germany. She lives on the lands of the Quw'utsun Hwulmuhw next to a creek in a cedar grove where she spends her time building community, dreaming, writing, and working as a counsellor and sex worker. She is a Reclaiming witch and co-organizer of Pleasures of Beltane and has been a life-long dreamer and magical practitioner.

Sophia Kirke: I'm a traditional witch dedicated to the path of Circe, living between the Alps and Andalusia in company with my dog. When not concocting teas and flower essences and collecting wild herbs and berries, I write short stories and poetry drawn from the island of my imagination, some of which involves transformation and shapeshifting. Occasionally, I make trips to the underworld, guided by Circe.

Terrance Gamble is a Mediterranean polytheist who has been studying witchcraft since his adolescence. An initiate in the Ophic Strix Tradition founded by Oracle Hekataios, he devotes much time honoring Hekate and Dionysus, as well as studying divination. He has also studied Black Rose Witchcraft and is a California Freemason and tarot reader. Terrance is also a watercolor artist and oil painter who creates devotional pieces for the many spirits he honors in his spiritual and magical practices.

Victoria Raschke has written four novels in the *Voices of the Dead* series and a companion recipe and spellbook, *Renegade Tea* (2021). The first novel in the *Verity Green: art & magic* series was released in 2023. She and her family founded 1000Volt Press in 2020 to publish the books they would like to see in the world and together they produce the *WitchLit* podcast which Victoria hosts.

Serpents of Circe

Vittorio Benetti is an Italian High Priest and Ordained Minister within the Temple of Witchcraft Tradition. He is actively working to build an Italian community by organizing public rituals and offering Witchcraft, Reiki, and meditation classes while partnering with Local Spirits. Apart from his spiritual roles, he has a diverse background as a musician in a punk band, known by the name Evil Vick. His involvement in the punk scenes and his experiences with the occupied social centers in Italy contributed to his commitment and his enduring interest in social issues and activism. He can be found on Instagram @vittoriobenettihp

A Manual to Magical Resilience

Resources

IN ADDITION TO THE RESOURCES that were compiled for *The New Aradia* and *The Gorgon's Guide*, we'd like to bring to your attention some newer publications that may be of interest to you, listed in no particular order:

- *Braiding Sweetgrass: Indigenous Wisdom, Scientific Knowledge and the Teachings of Plants* by Robin Wall Kimmerer
- *The Witch's Kin: Deepening Your Relationship with Nature, Spirits, and Humankind* by Asa West
- *Saving Democracy: A User's Manual for Every American* by David Pepper
- *Your Heart Was Made For This: Contemplative Practices for Meeting a World in Crisis with Courage, Integrity, and Love* by Oren Jay Sofer
- *Nourishing Resistance: Stories of Food, Protest, and Mutual Aid* by Wren Awry and Cindy Milstein
- *Overcoming Burnout* by Nicole Rose (ebook version only)
- *The Prisoner's Herbal* by Nicole Rose (ebook version only)
- *The White Deer: Ecospirituality and the Mythic* by Melinda Reidinger
- *Love in the Age of Ecological Apocalypse* by Carolyn Baker
- *Chronically Magickal: Navigating Chronic Illness with Witchcraft* by Danielle Dionne
- *Sacred Tears: A Witch's Guide to Grief* by Courtney Weber

FORTHCOMING RELEASES IN 2025 TO KEEP ON YOUR RADAR:

- *Queer Rites: A Magickal Grimoire to Honor Your Milestones with Pride* by Enfys J. Book
- *Slow Magic: Cultivate Lasting Transformation through Spellwork and Self-Growth* by Anthony Rella

www.ingramcontent.com/pod-product-compliance
Lightning Source LLC
Chambersburg PA
CBHW060532080526
44586CB00012B/710